CHURCH SURVEYS OF CHICHESTER ARCHDEACONRY
1602, 1610 & 1636

Interior of Upmarden Church
structurally unaltered: like the interiors inspectors would have encountered, but with more modern furnishings

CHURCH SURVEYS OF CHICHESTER ARCHDEACONRY 1602, 1610 & 1636

EDITED BY JOAN BARHAM AND ANDREW FOSTER

SUSSEX RECORD SOCIETY
VOLUME 98

Issued to members of the Society for the year 2016

Published 2018 by
Sussex Record Society
Barbican House,
High Street,
Lewes,
East Sussex, BN7 1YE.

Printed by Hobbs the Printers Ltd., Totton, Hampshire

VOLUMES ISSUED BY THE SUSSEX RECORD SOCIETY

In print volumes marked with an asterisk can be obtained from the Sussex Record Society, Barbican House, Lewes, East Sussex, BN7 1YE or through the Society's website: www.sussexrecordsociety.org

CONTENTS

cont...

For information on the church illustrations placed in the main text, please see Editorial
Policy and Notes on Illustrations (p li)

ACKNOWLEDGEMENTS

We are grateful to the following for permission to reproduce documents and images in this volume: to the Right Reverend Dr Martin Warner, Bishop of Chichester, for the use of ecclesiastical records now in the care of the West Sussex Record Office; to County Archivist Wendy Walker and the staff of that record office; and to the Sussex Archaeological Society for permission to reproduce images from the Sharpe Collection.

Joan Barham would like to pay particular thanks to Helen Poole, then of the SAS at Michelham Priory, who first gave her permission to photograph material from the Sharpe Collection when working on her thesis before 2010. Joan would also like to thank the archivists at WSRO who informed her of the uncatalogued cardboard box (Accession 9822) containing photographs, many unidentified, the 'treasure trove' from Archdeacon Walker's visitation. We would both like to thank Michael Moriarty for his help and advice on objects to be found in Chichester Cathedral Treasury. More specific thanks to clergy who have kindly given permission for reproduction of pictures of their church plate may be found amongst the inserted section of photographs in the text.

The production of any record society volume is a team effort, none more so than this one. Peter Wilkinson has been an unfailing source of advice, as has Caroline Adams, who contributed the final transcript of the entries for 1636. Peter produced the table that revealed analysis of when certificates were submitted for work completed on repairs requested in 1602; he also helped to unravel how the material for 1636 may have related to Archbishop Laud's Metropolitical visitation of 1635.

The most important 'editor' in many senses has been Roger Pearce, without whom this volume would not have materialised. He has compiled this volume superbly and supplied the index; we are deeply indebted to his ingenuity in manipulating text and photographs so expertly. And he has been unfailing in his encouragement, patience and support as the volume has slowly taken shape and been revised many times in the final stages.

Members of our local 'Early Modern Studies Group' have kindly discussed aspects of the work with us over several years, and given support in reading sections of material and commenting on supporting apparatus. This group has included: Caroline Adams, John Hawkins, Graham Claydon, Haighleagh Winslade, Hilary Caws, Helen Whittle, Jude Jones, Fiona McCall, Valerie Hitchman and Audrey Hamilton. Thanks should also go to members of a conference sponsored by Essex University, convened by Tom Freeman,

Amanda Flather and Justin Colson, at which Andrew Foster gave a paper on these surveys in 2016.

Trevor Cooper, Kenneth Fincham and Peter Wilkinson have proffered expert advice on the introduction, as has Michael Questier, who has given wise counsel on matters Roman Catholic in West Sussex and been a great source of encouragement. Our respective spouses, Jon and Julia have also been pillars of support and sources of constructive criticism, and we thank them wholeheartedly for what they have put up with while this volume has been compiled. Jon and Joan worked magnificently together on the production of the church diagram (Illustration 8) based on a very rough sketch by Andrew Foster. Finally, we would like to thank members of the Council of the Sussex Record Society for commissioning this volume.

INTRODUCTION:
CHURCH SURVEYS OF CHICHESTER ARCHDEACONRY 1602, 1610 & 1636

This introduction is designed to serve several purposes. First, it aims to provide an explanation of the documents that have been transcribed to form the main text of the volume, how the material was produced and why, and to be clear about what is included and what is not. Second, it will attempt to provide useful context, both locally and nationally, so that readers may gauge the significance of the material, and hence why it has been deemed worthy of publication by the Sussex Record Society. Third, it is hoped that the introduction will pose a number of questions and puzzles about what the material reveals about the state of the Church of England in the early seventeenth century, whilst also providing ample technical apparatus for those wishing to pursue matters further. The aim is to provide sufficient to whet the appetite for the documents that follow, give essential context to aid understanding, suggest where further research is necessary, but not to curtail the enjoyment – which we hope readers will have – when they analyse this material for themselves.

This volume provides transcriptions of church surveys conducted within the archdeaconry of Chichester during the first four decades of the seventeenth century. In crude terms the archdeaconry covered most of what is now deemed to be West Sussex and was divided into four rural deaneries: Storrington, Boxgrove, Midhurst and Arundel.[1] Church repair cases were presented fairly routinely to the diocesan courts, but what we have transcribed stems from three special surveys – one instigated by an archbishop, the other two by the diocesan bishops. This may be confirmed partly from the sheer volume of cases noted, as in 1610, and also from the production of special registers for the surveys of 1602 and 1636.[2]

The first survey quite clearly stemmed from a special commission, for it was authorised by John Whitgift, Archbishop of Canterbury in June 1602. He called for the survey to be conducted on an archidiaconal basis within all of the 27 dioceses of the two provinces of Canterbury and York that covered England and Wales.[3] In Sussex, this request for information yielded evidence that has survived for 133 churches and chapels within the archdeaconry of Chichester, including a further 19 churches in the peculiars of Chichester and of Pagham and Tarring, bringing the total to 152 churches and chapels.[4] This represents all

---

[1] See map of the parishes of the archdeaconry plxxiii.

[2] WSRO: Ep. I/17/13/ff.84-115; Ep. I/26/1; Ep. I/26/2.

[3] Appendix 1 gives Archbishop Whitgift's letter of June 1602; the island diocese of Sodor & Man, part of York province, is included in the total of 27 noted above.

[4] WSRO: Ep. I/26/1 contains material for the archdeaconry; Ep. III/6/Box 407/folder 3/25 gives details of the nine churches within and around Chichester under the Dean's jurisdiction; Ep. IV/2/8/ff.21r-24r provides material on the

Illustration 1: Archbishop John Whitgift (from the frontispiece of Strype, 1718)

bar half a dozen of the churches and chapels contained within the archdeaconry, itself a comment on the success of Archbishop Whitgift's initiative.

The inclusion of peculiar or exempt jurisdictions is a bonus in these surveys, for it provides evidence on more churches than might be expected in normal times. Peculiars were individual parishes, or more commonly groups of parishes, that for historical reasons were under the control of some authority other than the diocesan bishop.[5] In Chichester's case this entailed the Archbishop of Canterbury's Peculiar of Pagham and Tarring, a total of ten parishes in all, and,

---

10 churches of the Archbishop of Canterbury's Peculiar of Pagham & Tarring. See later for discussion of what happened for the archdeaconry of Lewes.

[5]   See glossary of terms; and for more comment on the diocesan background: Foster, A., 'Chichester diocese in the seventeenth century', *SAC*, 123, 1985, 187-94.

closer to home, the Peculiar of the Dean of Chichester, a total of nine parishes within and around the city of Chichester.[6] Peculiars affected around 11% of the parishes of England and Wales, and while they complicated administration, they were not such a problem as often thought, for – as here in Chichester diocese – they were largely in the control of other ecclesiastical authorities.[7] Over in the east, the archbishop also possessed the Peculiar of South Malling, while the town of Battle was the fiefdom of a Dean of Battle.[8] From the point of view of bishops, however, peculiars were a nuisance, for they were usually exempt from visitations by them or their archdeacons, and thus difficult to police. Moreover, what records they created might sometimes be lodged in different registries from those of the diocese. Their inclusion in 1602 is a further indication of Archbishop Whitgift's desire to secure as complete a survey as possible.

Regardless of the administrative difficulties posed by the existence of peculiars, it is doubtful if any bishop or diocesan chancellor of this period would have been able to give a precise figure for the number of churches and chapels contained within any given diocese or archdeaconry. That would depend on agreement on how chapels were to be regarded, the extent of any major building renovations going on at the time, and even temporary changes in use or later amalgamations. In the survey commenced in 1602 we lack evidence for: the chapel of Burton, usually associated with Coates; Egdean, which was in the process of reconstruction only completed in 1622; and Stopham, Rogate and Pulborough.[9] Yet, to miss evidence on only five churches represents a huge achievement for the authorities at the time.[10] Estimates of how many churches should have come within the jurisdiction of dioceses at this time are further complicated by rival claims, as Puritan critics sought to exaggerate the number of livings without a preaching ministry, while those in authority tried to play down those figures.[11] Hence estimates for the diocese of Chichester as a whole varied between roughly 250 and 300 livings.[12] In the *Liber Cleri* produced for Archbishop Abbot's Metropolitical visitation of 1615, he was informed of 150 churches in the four deaneries and two peculiars within the archdeaconry of Chichester, and these

---

[6] See bibliography for material checked for the peculiars and for more on the nature of their records: *Diocese of Chichester: A Catalogue of the Records of the Bishop, Archdeacons and Former Exempt Jurisdictions*, compiled by Francis Steer and Isabel Kirby, WSCC, 1966.

[7] The full significance of peculiar or exempt jurisdictions will be discussed in Foster, A., forthcoming, *Dioceses of England and Wales, c.1540-1700*, in two volumes, one comprising a catalogue of diocesan records for the whole country.

[8] *Diocese of Chichester Catalogue*, xxiii, 154-161, 189-191.

[9] WSRO: Ep. I/26/1; the church list indicates for which dates we possess surveys, and thus where evidence is missing; it includes dates for which WSRO holds glebe terriers relating to these churches, chiefly 1615 and 1635, and also indicates rectories and provides a rough guide to the value of the livings.

[10] There are of course puzzles as to why material for these churches has not survived, particularly the relatively important market town of Pulborough, the only church for which we lack information for any of the three surveys; see discussion of this matter later.

[11] See Foster, A., 'Chichester diocese', *SAC*, 123, 188.

[12] *Ibid.*

incorporated associated chapels like Ashington with Buncton, and Greatham with Wiggonholt.[13]

The second batch of material, or survey, stems from the autumn primary visitation of Bishop Samuel Harsnett, and the initial reports are contained within the detection book covering October to December 1610.[14] This provides material on 107 churches and chapels, a lower figure than before, illustrating that even an incoming bishop conducting his primary visitation – at which he would expect respect and a high degree of compliance from his clergy and churchwardens – could not match the authority of an archbishop.[15] Harsnett's survey does not contain material on the ten parishes of the archbishop's Peculiar of Pagham and Tarring, but it does afford details of five of the city churches, where the bishop's authority – perhaps because this was his primary visitation – seems to have overruled the Dean's, yet curiously, not for the entire Chichester deanery.[16]

The third tranche of material on churches is found in the returns for what must surely have been the archdeacon's Michaelmas visitation, carried out under the watchful eye of Bishop Richard Montagu and conducted in the autumn of 1636. Yet this is assuredly related to the earlier work of Archbishop William Laud's Metropolitical visitation of 1635, about which we sadly have only fragments of information.[17] The 1636 survey yields excellent descriptions of churches and chapels for 125 places, but unfortunately omits information on the 19 churches of the two peculiars within the region. It may also be significant that this visitation covers fewer churches than that of 1602, possibly because of resistance provoked by the slightly more ideological thrust of the questions of those in authority in the 1630s.[18] Whereas Whitgift was concerned to check the basic fabric and fittings of the churches, Montagu and his colleagues were more

---

[13] WSRO: Ep. I/18/32.
[14] WSRO: Ep. I/17/13/ff. 84-115; we are grateful to Professor Kenneth Fincham who first alerted us to this run of cases many years ago, about which he wrote in *Prelate as Pastor, The Episcopate of James I*, 1990, 138-9. The acts or decisions of the summary or 'office' procedures of the bishop's consistory court were recorded in act books, most frequently known as detection books.
[15] The list of 107 might have been 113, but the representatives of six churches failed to provide evidence on the day and were simply cited to provide their list of defects and amend accordingly: Amberley, Climping, Ferring, Poling, Terwick and Wiston; Pulborough was just left blank.
[16] Peculiars came in many shapes and sizes. Some held exemption from the authority of the ordinary for all time; others might be subject to that of a primary visitation, while others might be subject to a Metropolitical visitation. Local practice, as at Chichester, might waive authority in favour of local surrogates, as when the Archbishop of Canterbury delegated the administration of his Peculiar of Pagham and Tarring to Bishop Harsnett between 1610 and 1619: *Diocese of Chichester Catalogue*, 239-40. So why do we not have material for that peculiar?
[17] WSRO: Ep. I/26/2; see appendix 12 regarding visitations of the diocese.
[18] Discussed more fully later; compare the tone of the articles supplied in appendices 4, 9 & 11. At Norwich, Bishop Montagu commenced his articles on churches with a quotation from Haggai I.4: 'Is it time for you, O ye, to dwell in ceiled houses, and the house of the Lord to lie waste?' as found in *Visitation Articles and Injunctions of the Early Stuart Church, II*, ed. Fincham, K., COERS, 1998, 191. This quotation drew from the Elizabethan homily on care of churches.

Illustration 2: Archbishop Laud (from the frontispiece of Laud, 1695)

interested in the furniture and fittings, particularly those associated with communion tables and fonts, matters which aroused old fears of Popery in some people.[19] Alas, it should not be concluded that this meant that churches were necessarily in any better state of general repair in the 1630s than they had been in 1602.[20]

The nature and purpose of the sources

The surveys were essentially all compiled in the same manner, relying on standard visitation practice, which placed responsibility firmly with incumbents

---

[19] Fletcher, A., *A County Community in Peace and War: Sussex 1600-1660*,1975; see appendix 11 for a copy of Montagu's Visitation Articles employed with minor variations in this diocese between 1628 and 1638.
[20] See cautionary tale of Slindon discussed later.

and churchwardens to report faults under oath.[21] The visitation process commenced with the issue of 'Articles of Enquiry' produced by the bishop or archdeacon, which churchwardens had to purchase and then answer.[22] In the later survey of 1724, commissioners were employed to visit the churches, and Canon 86 of the Canons of 1604 facilitated that possibility.[23] When at York, Archbishop Neile lamented in an annual report to King Charles I, that 'the Bishop can but enquire by the oaths of Churchwardens and Sidesmen, who make no conscience of dispensing with their othe, and can hardly be brought to present any thing, be thinges never so farr out of order'.[24] This in turn seems to have echoed the King's own concerns noted in his proclamation of 1629.[25] This was an imperfect system from the outset.

While we have no clear evidence of named commissioners being used, the survey for 1636 stands apart from the other two in content and form, and does raise suspicions that some churches were visited rather than reliance being placed solely on cross-examination of churchwardens. This could well have been done in accordance with standard visitation practice, for inspections might have been carried out by the archdeacon and/or his official, or by carefully selected local clergy from the deanery in question, just as a few reliable men were licensed to preach across an archdeaconry or a whole diocese. Certainly the 1636 survey suggests very tight questioning of churchwardens and clergymen against prepared criteria.[26] The surveys are more uniform, focused on interior furnishings and things necessary for the conduct of services, and get couched in the form of a series of orders. Even the crossings out that occur more frequently in this document might be interpreted as a check list in which certain items were not found to be wanting, as opposed to having been sorted by a later date.[27] These crossings out occur more frequently than the few scribal errors of the first two surveys. The telling scrap of evidence creating doubts about the process

---

[21] Marchant, R., *The Church Under the Law*, 1969, 114-46 provides a clear account of the visitation process based on practice in the Province of York.

[22] See copies of Visitation Articles with their slightly different emphases, yet all based on the Canons of the Church of England: appendices 4, 9 & 11. A normal visitation would usually entail the assembly of clergy and churchwardens to meet visitors at the main church of their rural deanery, where they would submit their replies and some matters would be dealt with 'summarily', while others would require reporting to sessions of the Consistory court held in Chichester.

[23] Ford, W., ed., *Chichester Diocesan Surveys 1686 and 1724*, SRS, 78, 1994; appendix 6 contains Canon 86, which begs questions about why this device was not employed in the diocese of Chichester as far as we can see.

[24] 'Annual Accounts of the Church of England, 1632-1639', ed. Fincham, K., in *From the Reformation to the permissive society*, ed. Barber, M., Taylor, S., & Sewell, G., Church of England Record Society, XVIII, 2010, Archbishop Neile's report on York province for 1633, 93. So concerned was he about the reliability of his Metropolitical visitation, that Neile employed roving commissioners to report back to his Chancery Court, through which over 100 churches were found to be defective. For details of church campaigns in York province see: Foster, A., 'Church Policies of the 1630s', in *Conflict in Early Stuart England*, ed. Cust, R., & Hughes, A., 1989, 193-223.

[25] Appendix 8.

[26] See discussion of results later and 1636 material found in the surveys.

[27] See discussion of our approach to the transcritions in editorial notes.

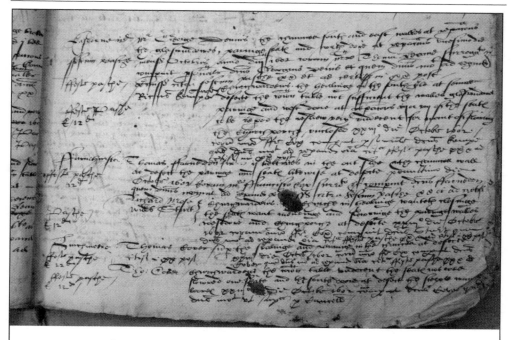

Illustration 3: Sample of 1602 Survey: Easebourne, Fernhurst, Linchmere

comes in the entry for Buncton, where 'John Peter the chappell warden appeared himselfe but brought not the key to the chappell soe that we could goe in to view it.[28]

To return, however, to what we think was the more likely common process: on making their statements under oath, those responsible for the chancels, and the churchwardens responsible for the naves, were given the task of completing repairs by a stipulated time, which usually involved appearing in court again to 'certify' that work had been completed.[29] They appeared at courts held in Chichester Cathedral, usually presided over by surrogates working for the bishops and their diocesan chancellors.[30] The court for the Peculiar of Pagham and Tarring was held at All Saints, Chichester, which was in the Pallant.[31] The surveys of both 1602 and 1636 were clearly deemed to be important enough to justify the compilation of separate volumes of registers, the earlier of which

---

[28] See entry for Buncton.
[29] See glossary of terms and later discussion.
[30] See section that follows on key people involved in these surveys.
[31] Chichester was essentially divided into four quadrants within the old walls, one of them was the Palatine jurisdiction of the Archbishop of Canterbury, hence the name Pallant, another was basically the jurisdiction of the Cathedral Dean and Chapter, and the other two were under the control of the city burghers, but still liable to general ecclesiastical jurisdiction.

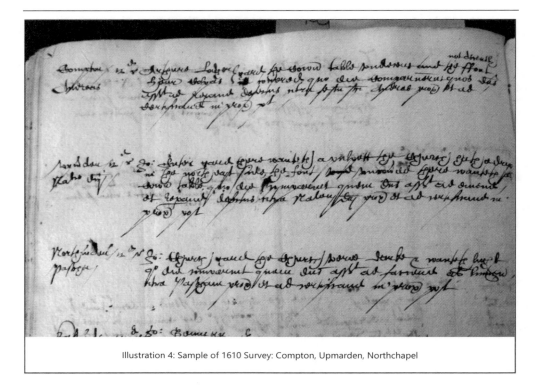

Illustration 4: Sample of 1610 Survey: Compton, Upmarden, Northchapel

contained details of how cases were pursued.[32] In 1610 the material is simply found in a run of cases within an ordinary detection book in which more routine business also intruded.[33] Again, however, the progress of the cases towards production of certificates may be pursued over later months. Timelines of these church cases, including contextual material, may be found in appendices to this volume.[34]

The court material is not easy to read, being written in a cramped and abbreviated secretary hand. The well-known historian, Geoffrey Elton, opined that:

'the act books of the Church courts are among the most strikingly repulsive of all the relics of the past – written in cramped and hurried hands, in very abbreviated and technical Latin, often preserved (if that is the right word) in fairly noisome conditions, ill-sorted and mostly unlisted, unindexed and sometimes broken in pieces.'[35]

---

[32] Hence WSRO: Ep. I/26/1 & 2 catalogued separately as church surveys together with Ep. I/26/3 for Bishop Bower's survey of 1724 published for the *SRS* by W.K.Ford in 1994.

[33] WSRO: Ep.1/17/13, ff. 84-115.

[34] Appendices 2, 7, & 10.

[35] Elton, G., *England 1200-1640 The Sources of History*, 1969, 104-5.

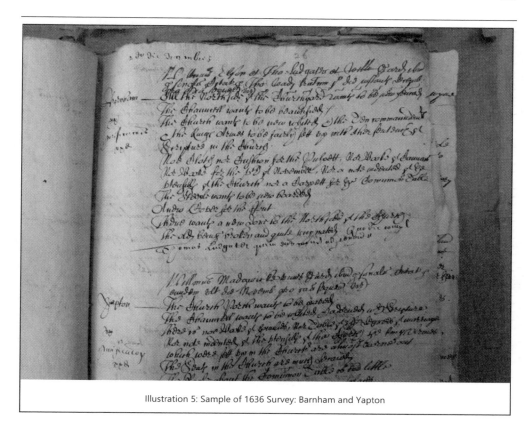

Illustration 5: Sample of 1636 Survey: Barnham and Yapton

He warned that 'only young scholars, still enthusiastic, physically strong, and possessed of a sound digestion, are advised to tackle these materials.'[36] Conditions have clearly improved since he wrote, but unfortunately, on consulting the original manuscript for 1602-3 in writing this volume, that book was found to be in need of major repair, and parts of the tops and bottoms of the document were badly torn. It has since been the subject of an expensive, delicate and time-consuming conservation project.[37] The other two surveys are in better condition, although both have also presented palaeographical difficulties.[38]

It has already been noted that the 'surveys' fall into different forms. The volume for 1602 consists of 34ff in all, the first part of which (ff.1-18) contains the reports on the different churches taken by deanery. The second part (ff.20-33) records in abbreviated form the consistory court sessions to which churchwardens and impropriators reported to sign off on completion of repairs, or in some cases, to

---

[36] Ibid., 105.

[37] One positive outcome of work on this volume has been a generous subvention by the Council of the SRS toward the cost of conserving this valuable document.

[38] See illustrations of each of the documents concerned.

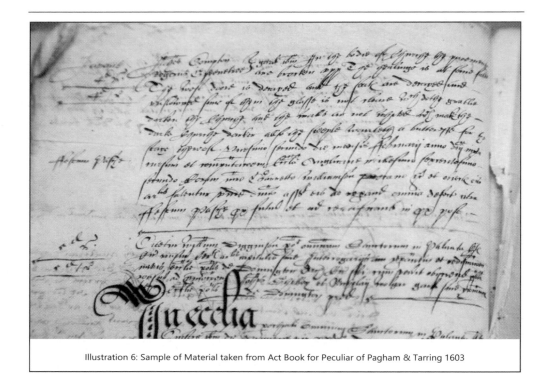

Illustration 6: Sample of Material taken from Act Book for Peculiar of Pagham & Tarring 1603

be excommunicated for failure to do so.[39] The courts ran from May 1603 until the last one noted in March 1604. Our text has been transcribed from the detailed surveys, while the court technicalities contained in the second part have formed the basis of both a detailed summary of when cases were signed off, or not, together with a general timescale pertinent to these events.[40] The survey of 1610 appears within a standard detection book for the archdeaconry. To follow up the certificates one simply proceeds through the cases that occur until they peter out after Easter of 1611.[41] The survey for 1636 again forms a separate volume, in this case of 37ff, again moving through the deaneries and covering a period from November to December 1636.[42] Details of when people were expected to appear in court were noted in the margins, and were mostly given as the Feast of the Purification, 2 February. Unlike the volume for 1602, no details are given of later court hearings prompted by these cases.[43]

---

[39] WSRO: Ep. I/26/1; see appendices 2 & 5.
[40] Appendices 2 & 5.
[41] WSRO: Ep. I/17/13.
[42] WSRO: Ep. I/26/2.
[43] It has been deemed beyond our scope for this volume, but court entries relating to business first raised in the surveys of 1610 and 1636, could be pursued over several years amongst the full range of cases covered by the diocesan detection books, as the example of Slindon discussed later reveals.

The list of churches covered in the three surveys for the Archdeaconry of Chichester reveals a number of puzzles. While the majority of churches are covered for our three dates of 1602, 1610 and 1636, clearly that does not apply to all. Nor does there appear to be any rhyme or reason as to the ones that are missing, apart from the peculiars. There is no obvious geographical pattern; it is not just a matter of chapels going missing; nor is there any correlation with poorer parishes. It could be that those churches failed to send representatives to the relevant courts, or that their cases were dealt with summarily on the occasion of a visit. This might apply to the rather strange and exceptional case of Pulborough (missing in all three surveys), where the incumbent in 1602 and 1610 was John Drury, the Diocesan Chancellor after 1606, (but already an important lawyer in the diocese in 1602); while in 1636 it was Archdeacon Lawrence Pay![44] Peculiar jurisdictions always posed problems, as already noted, and Archbishop Laud asked that especial care be taken to check on them in 1635, so it is probable that this is a case where the records were dutifully kept separately, and they have since been lost.[45] The material for both peculiars was kept separately for the survey of 1602. We are fortunate to possess evidence for five of the nine Chichester churches in 1610, but we have nothing similar for 1636.

The compilation of the surveys into separate volumes could provide a clue, for that might have facilitated losses of material once court officials felt they had used them to their satisfaction.[46] This would certainly apply to records produced for the peculiars as noted above, but it is lent credence by what we now know of the records of the archdeaconry of Lewes. It has long been thought that we had no evidence of a series of church surveys for that archdeaconry, although we do have the surviving returns for the different survey requested by Archbishop Whitgift in 1603, while those returns do not appear to have survived for Chichester.[47] This second survey is the one that has been beloved by population historians because it yielded numbers of the congregation, details on recusants, as well as material on impropriations.[48]

Close examination of the detection books for Lewes, however, reveals a 'shadow' of the church survey for 1602. The detection book covering 1600-1605 reveals churches being cited for defects, such as lacking a bible or Book of Common Prayer at St Michael in Lewes, or the church being 'weather beaten' at

---

[44] It is just possible that this church was treated more casually on the word of its illustrious incumbents, or that the reports did not merit documentation.

[45] See Appendix 9 with Archbishop Laud's instructions to his officials; checking for material at Lambeth has drawn a blank.

[46] Ordinary court books would be in constant use for checking on outcomes and then picking up new business; special volumes might be more easily laid aside and neglected.

[47] Renshaw, W.C. 'Ecclesiastical Returns for 81 parishes in East Sussex made in 1603', *SRS*, 4, 1905, 1-17. See appendix 3 for the details of this survey.

[48] Dyer, A., & Palliser, D., *The Diocesan Population Returns for 1563 and 1603*, 2005.

Hurstpierpoint, and lack of shingles for the steeple at Whatlington.[49] What follows in this detection book suggests a series of dates given for certificates, but without details of the surveys. The entries range from October 1602 until July 1603 and eventually seem to encompass 89 churches, well over half of the archdeaconry. The list does not include churches from the archbishop's peculiar of South Malling.[50] This suggests that surveys were indeed carried out for the Lewes Archdeaconry, just as for Chichester, and kept in separate volumes that have since been lost.[51] Close searching of extant Lewes material for the later surveys has sadly drawn a blank.[52]

Several points may perhaps usefully be drawn from comparison of the two surveys for Lewes archdeaconry carried out in the autumn of 1602 and again in 1603. First, both surveys covered churches drawn from across the whole archdeaconry. Secondly, both surveys yielded returns for over 80 churches and their congregations, which was after all the thrust of the second survey. Third, it looks as if 49 of those churches covered made returns to both surveys. And finally, if there is something to detect from this, it is that the bulk of the returns came for churches in Lewes and Pevensey deaneries (as one might expect given their size), but the deanery of Dallington that bordered on Kent was under-represented in both surveys. This might suggest some problems for the authorities in enforcement of policy at the far eastern end of the diocese.[53]

While the diocese of Chichester possesses an excellent collection of diocesan archives for the early modern period, possibly among the top six such collections held by record offices in the country, it is relevant here to comment on what else is missing in this 'jigsaw puzzle'.[54] We are fortunate to possess three 'snapshots' of the state of the churches in the early seventeenth century. Much more research could be carried out on the detection books of the diocese for which there is an excellent run, together with the separate court books for each peculiar.[55] This might help to establish a fuller picture of the fairly constant repair of churches over the decades. What is sadly missing is any direct evidence of the Metropolitical visitation conducted for Archbishop Bancroft in the summer of 1605, or for Archbishop Abbot's Metropolitical visitation conducted in the

---

[49] WSRO: Ep. II/9/9.
[50] *Ibid.*
[51] Extant Act books for the peculiar of South Malling cover the years 1613-32, but there is then a large gap until 1673: *Diocese of Chichester Catalogue*, 155. There is no evidence of this material having ended up in Lambeth Palace archives.
[52] See bibliography for details of material consulted.
[53] The whole question of what happened in Lewes archdeaconry clearly cries out for more research: the terrain of this area might be a factor in bad weather.
[54] This assessment is based on research for Foster, A.W., forthcoming, on the dioceses of England and Wales.
[55] See the bibliography for a sense of the riches of the archives and, of course, the *Diocese of Chichester Catalogue*.

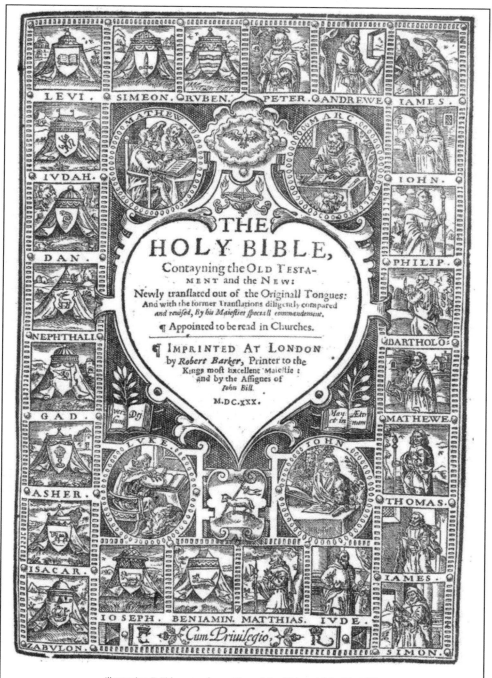

Illustration 7: Titlepage of an edition of the Bible published in 1630

summer of 1615.[56] And it has already been noted that we are working with fragments in relation to Archbishop Laud's Metropolitical visitation of 1635. These visitations would have carried great authority and we might have expected to find Bancroft as well as Laud showing concern for the state of parish churches and chapels. Rather than mourning what we have lost, however, what follows reveals why we should rejoice in what we possess.

Why do these church surveys merit publication?

The church surveys that survive for the Chichester Archdeaconry provide excellent detail on the churches and chapels in the early seventeenth century. The information gleaned complements that which we possess on the early eighteenth century, thanks to the more elaborate survey conducted for Bishop Bowers.[57] Chichester diocese stands out as being one of only three dioceses for which evidence of Whitgift's survey survives. The other two are Lincoln and Norwich; in other words, we possess such material for only three dioceses out of the 27 that covered England and Wales in the seventeenth century. Perhaps an even clearer way of expressing the significance of this is to say that we possess material for 1602 for only seven of the 62 archdeaconries of the whole country.[58]

Other dioceses hold useful church surveys for the early seventeenth century, notably Peterborough, Gloucester, Durham, York and Chester, but what makes the collections at Chichester of even greater value is that we possess material for later surveys, most notably that conducted in 1636.[59] This affords great scope for comparison and also sheds light on a range of ecclesiastical policies pursued during the reigns of James I and his son Charles.

Comparison of the rich material we possess in Sussex for 1602, 1610 and 1636 reveals the shift in interest from real concern for the basic upkeep of churches and chapels at the start of the century, to a new emphasis on fixtures and fittings within the buildings, and matters of ceremonial concern.[60] This highlights differences between the experience of Archbishop Whitgift, responsible for

---

[56] One important legacy of Abbot's visitation that does survive is an excellent run of glebe terriers for 1615; see church list.

[57] Ford, W.K., ed., *Chichester Diocesan Surveys 1686 and 1724*, SRS, 78, 1994.

[58] The seven archdeaconries that provide such records for 1602 are: Chichester, Norwich, Norfolk, Sudbury, Suffolk, Lincoln and Stowe.

[59] The best collection of church surveys per se is undoubtedly to be found at the Northamptonshire Record Office, which holds a run of seven volumes for the diocese of Peterborough from 1606 through to 1681, together with a survey for 1605 (Misc. Book 12); the only diocese for which we have a complete set for 1602 is Norwich: Norfolk Record Office: DN/EST 58/4/1-3 & DN/ MSC 1/24, 2/3.

[60] The bibliography provides details of excellent work produced on these themes by scholars such as Kenneth Fincham, Nicholas Tyacke, Trevor Cooper, Graham Parry, Julia Merritt and Valerie Hitchman. Peter Lake will shortly be producing a book on the themes he first discussed in 'The Laudian Style: Order, Uniformity and the Pursuit of the Beauty of Holiness in the 1630s', in *The Early Stuart Church*, ed. Fincham, K., 1993, 161-185.

guiding his Church of England in the latter years of Queen Elizabeth I, and the combined policies of Archbishop Laud and Charles I, who were both to be executed, partly owing to their particular vision of the Church of England: Laud in 1645 and Charles I in 1649.

This material is collectively deemed worthy of publication because it represents such an excellent account of Sussex churches for a relatively short period.[61] It permits detailed analysis of what was happening in the parishes under different episcopal administrations at a critical stage in the development of the Church of England, and picks out evidence of different liturgical concerns. Evidence of some of the changes that came about as a result of these findings may still be seen in many West Sussex churches to this day.[62] This material represents responses to different initiatives, but with a common focus on the state of the churches. While the surviving material for Whitgift's survey is rare, so too is that for the survey conducted in 1636, where the initiative is well known for many dioceses – seen to be highly representative of 'Laudianism' – but survival of material is also incomplete.[63] Excellent runs of material for Buckinghamshire and for Nottinghamshire have long been in print, for scholars and 'church crawlers' alike have always appreciated the value and importance of these surveys.[64]

We have provided a summary list of churches covered by the surveys and details are provided for 157 churches in all, not far short of a full complement of all the churches and chapels in the archdeaconry. 1602 yields material for 152 of these, while 1636 provides details of 125; 1610 gives the smallest number of the three sets with 107. This is still a respectable total and offers valuable comparative detail.[65] We are fortunate, however, as already noted, in being able to provide some details of groups of churches that commonly get neglected owing to loss of sources, namely those that fell into the peculiar jurisdictions.

The volume is arranged under parishes in alphabetical order for the whole archdeaconry, although the original material was collected by deaneries in response to the surveys of 1602 and 1636, less systematically for 1610.[66] It was

---

[61] It complements *SRS* volume 78 as already noted, and fulfills the ambition of Wyn K. Ford and Alan Dibben, who first spotted the significance of these surveys and hoped to publish them for SRS many years ago.

[62] See Joan Barham's photographs of Sussex churches today that still contain splendid examples of seventeenth-century church fittings; see also the excellent website: sussexparishchurches.org.

[63] For different views about what survives and its significance, compare and contrast: Davies, J., *The Caroline Captivity of the Church*, 1992, and Fincham, K., and Tyacke, N., *Altars Restored*, 2007.

[64] Brinkworth, E., 'The Laudian Church in Buckinghamshire", *University of Birmingham Historical Journal*, V, 1955, 31-59; Gibbs, R., 'The State of Buckinghamshire Churches in the 16th and 17th centuries', *Records of Buckinghamshire*, 6, 1887, 150-67, 245-58; Marchant, R., 'The Restoration of Nottinghamshire Churches, 1635-1640', *Transactions of the Thoroton Society*, LXV, 1961, 58-93.

[65] The material relating to the reports for 1610 provides much less detail than the other two surveys, as will be seen in the text provided for each church.

[66] See earlier discussion of the process by which these documents were made.

felt that it would be preferable for readers to see the entries for the churches on one page rather than take each survey separately. It was also felt useful to supply contextual material, where possible, indicating the deanery for regional location, names of incumbents during the period, and the patrons of the livings where known. A useful feature for 1602 is that names of those to whom the impropriation was 'farmed out' were often given, indicating those who took the 'great' or rectorial tithes, and thus took responsibility for the upkeep of the chancel.[67] This will help those who wish to allocate responsibility for the various failings in church repairs, bearing in mind that it is only the 1602 survey that gives us such full details separately for chancels and naves.[68] One further embellishment lies with the photographs supplied that are drawn from material held by the Sussex Archaeological Society and the West Sussex Record Office, or were taken by Joan Barham in the course of her study of the impact of the Reformation on the diocese of Chichester as a whole.[69] These represent another sound justification for this volume, for they draw on sources of which Sussex is justifiably proud, having an excellent run of artists and photographers who have painted and photographed Sussex churches over the past three centuries.[70]

Why was there such concern about the state of parish churches and chapels?

Given the relative success of the Church of England as an institution since, it is easy to forget that the 'Elizabethan Church Settlement' that emerged after 1559 – the much-heralded 'via media' – was not terribly stable or well founded in practice. The acts of Supremacy and Uniformity, and then the 39 Articles, provided a basic identity that it would be unwise yet to claim as 'Anglicanism'. Richard Hooker's *Laws of Ecclesiastical Polity* provided a greater intellectual justification much later in the reign. In practice, however, the Queen neglected her bishops and senior clergy, left sees vacant for many years, suspended one Archbishop, Grindal, and only allowed her last, Whitgift, to sit on her Privy Council. She also presided over a further period of spoliation of church property that was only brought to a halt by her successor James VI and I in 1604.[71]

---

[67] See glossary of terms.
[68] See Canons noted in appendix 6.
[69] See editorial notes for more about the photographs; for Joan Barham's thesis see the bibliography.
[70] The centenary volume of the SRS, *Sussex Depicted Views and Descriptions 1600-1800*, ed. Farrant, J., 85, 2001 celebrated earlier aspects of this tradition. For more on how we have dealt with the entries and the photographs see our editorial notes.
[71] This topic provided the *raison d'etre* for Christopher Hill's great work, *Economic Problems of the Church*, 1956; modified later by O'Day, R. & Heal, F., *Princes & Paupers in the English Church 1500-1800*, 1981; Heal, F., *Of Prelates and Princes*, 1980; for a return to this theme recently see: Foster, A., 'Bishops, Church and State, c.1530-1646' in *The Oxford History of Anglicanism*, I, ed. A. Milton, OUP, 2017, 84-102.

At parish level, incumbents and churchwardens were left largely to fend for themselves.[72] The turnover of clergy between 1559 and 1562 was such that large numbers of parishes were bereft of incumbents for much of the first decade of her reign. Pluralities and non-residence were common, and remained much cited abuses throughout the reign. The shock of the Reformation had a profound effect on the upkeep of parish churches, which now lost a panoply of support that had previously been provided when guilds and chantry priests buttressed the work of churchwardens in sustaining church repairs.[73] Puritan petitions concerning the lack of a godly ministry – the full supply of an educated, preaching ministry – spilled over into other reports that many parish churches were falling down.[74] There was a feeling that this was also part of a general economic crisis for the church in that many livings had fallen into the hands of lay impropriators; hence the authorities were interested in seeing how chancels in particular were faring in 1602.[75] Such reports prompted Archbishop Whitgift to act and to take the unusual step of commissioning a complete survey of the dioceses, for he was worried that the Queen had 'been enformed that divers churches and chauncells within this realme are gratelie decayed and some of them either falne downe or lyke to fall down'.[76]

Whitgift's letter was dispatched from Lambeth Palace on 21 June 1602 and acted upon over the next twelve months. [77] The bulk of the survey in West Sussex was carried out between September and November 1602, with stragglers noted as late as June 1603.[78] Although we know of no direct connection, it is probable that these surveys influenced Whitgift, Bancroft and others in the compiling of the Canons that were ratified by Convocation and Parliament in 1604, in which there were strong sections relating to the care of churches and responsibilities of the churchwardens.[79] The concern with the effect of impropriations is picked up in a second important letter issued by Archbishop Whitgift in 1603, probably when positioning himself to answer questions from the new king regarding the state

---

[72] Haigh, C., 'The Taming of the Reformation: Preachers, Pastors and Parishioners in Elizabethan and Early Stuart England', *History*, 85, 2000, 572-88.

[73] Duffy, E., *The Voices of Morebath*, 2001; Kumin, B., *The Shaping of a Community*, 1996; Burgess, C., 'The Pre-Reformation Churchwardens' Accounts and Parish Government: Lessons from London and Bristol, *English Historical Review*, cxix, 480, 2004, 87-116.

[74] Babbage, S., *Puritanism and Richard Bancroft*, 1962 is strong on the petitions; Foster, 'Chichester Diocese', *SAC*, 123, 187-94; Collinson, P., 'The Elizabethan Church and the new religion', in *The Reign of Elizabeth I*, ed. Haigh, C., 1984, 169-94.

[75] Hill, C., *Economic Problems of the Church*, 1956; this work was soon modified by the work of Felicity Heal and Claire Cross, and more recently by the findings of Brett Usher, *William Cecil and Episcopacy, 1559-1577*, 2003. The view that lay impropriators were not pulling their weight has been challenged recently in the work of Lucy Kaufman, 'Ecclesiastical Improvements, Lay Impropriations and the Building of a Post-Reformation church in England, 1560-1600,' *Historical Journal*, 2015, 1-23.

[76] Appendix 1.

[77] *Ibid.*

[78] Appendix 5.

[79] Appendix 6.

of the Church, at the same time as Puritan agitators presented James with their Millenary Petition.[80] These were difficult times for those in authority in the Church of England, uncertain as they must have been about how the King would react. Their concerns were eventually allayed by events at the Hampton Court Conference held early in 1604, and the commissioning of Bancroft to pursue the drawing up of new Canons for the Church of England in Convocation.[81]

What followed in the reign of James I has been described as something of a renaissance.[82] Evidence is mounting that major campaigns to improve the state of parish churches were conducted between 1603 and 1625, a period often thought of as one of neglect before the arrival of Archbishop Laud in 1633 – a story he was keen to promote when talking about his predecessor, Archbishop Abbot.[83] Samuel Harsnett, who became Bishop of Chichester in 1609, was something of a maverick, yet he held strong views that aligned him with a group known as 'Arminians', who favoured order and ceremony and a return to many ways regarded as 'Popish' and thus feared by Puritans. He was also a rather irascible, difficult man who was not particularly popular in any of the places where he held responsibility.[84] He was accused of financial incompetence while Master of Pembroke College, Cambridge and was later cited in Parliament in 1624 for his divisive actions when Bishop of Norwich. He soon fell out with the mayor and civic elite of Chichester and wrote to friends that he preferred his residence in Aldingbourne for that reason.[85] He was not part of the main group of Arminians associated with Richard Neile and William Laud, the so-called 'Durham House' group, although he was trusted with being Archbishop of York in 1629, where he also showed concern for the churches of his province.[86] He died in 1631 before he could achieve much there.

One distinguishing feature of the Arminians was their concern for the state of churches and cathedrals, for due reverence for the buildings (including a revival of interest in consecration services), and emphasis on proper ceremonial

---

[80] Appendix 3.

[81] For classic versions of this story: Usher, R., *The Reconstruction of the English Church*, II vols., 1910, and Babbage, S., *Puritanism and Richard Bancroft*, 1962.

[82] Yule, G., 'James VI and I: furnishing the churches in his two kingdoms', *Religion, Culture and Society in Early Modern Britain*, ed., Fletcher, A. & Roberts, P., 1994; MacCulloch, D., 'The Myth of the English Reformation', *Journal of British Studies*, 30, 1991, 1-19.

[83] This view of Abbot as a lax archbishop is echoed in Clarendon's monumental *History of the Rebellion and Civil Wars in England*, 3 vols., 1702-4, I, 68-9, and also in Hugh Trevor-Roper's celebrated, over indulgent attack on the Jacobean bench of bishops, 'King James and his bishops,' *History Today*, Sept., 1955, 571-81.

[84] *ODNB*: Harsnett; Foster, 'Chichester diocese', *SAC*; Foster, A., 'Bishops of Chichester 1503-1709', in *Chichester – The Palace and its Bishops*, Otter Memorial Papers, 27, 2011, 167-74.

[85] Harsnett wrote sourly of the 'unsavoury government of Chichester', which he also accused of being 'puritanically addicted': Foster, Chichester diocese, SAC, 192.

[86] *ODNB*: Durham House Group.

regarding communion and baptism.[87] They stressed the importance of communion tables as 'altars', which they preferred to be railed in to prevent abuse.[88] These issues had not become prominent when Harsnett first obtained Chichester in 1609, but he followed the leading scholar of the Arminian movement to the diocese, namely Lancelot Andrewes.[89] And Andrewes too had started to show an interest in the state of churches in his short period as Bishop of Chichester, even though he was scarcely ever down here in the diocese.[90] Harsnett's primary visitation conducted in 1610 led to a series of presentments that filtered through to the church courts over the next two years, sufficient for us to say that they represent another 'survey'. This is similar to the evidence of activity that we find in other dioceses such as Gloucester, Durham and Peterborough.[91] Yet the concerns picked up in 1610 are closer to those matters detected in 1602 than those revealed in 1636.

Arminian influences gained sway in the Church by the 1630s, when Archbishops Neile and Laud came to preside over the two provinces of York and Canterbury. They authorised major campaigns to take better care of churches, the one initiated in York province eventually encompassing over 600 churches.[92] They were aided in these initiatives by royal support from Charles I, demonstrated earlier in a Royal Proclamation of 1629 calling for better care of churches.[93] King Charles I had been carefully alerted to problems, much as the Queen had been primed in 1602, or James I in 1603. Soon after, a Commission for the repair of St Paul's Cathedral in 1631 adopted that place as a flagship for the cause of church restoration campaigns around the country.[94] All clergy, including those in Sussex, were encouraged to raise funds for St Paul's, and a report for Chichester diocese indicates that over £50 was so raised from the clergy of the archdeaconry of Chichester in 1634, while around £38 was forthcoming from the archdeaconry of Lewes.[95] Over £89 was raised from the clergy of the diocese a year later.[96]

The Archdeacon of Chichester's visitation of 1636 may thus be placed in the context of a growing Arminian interest in the condition and restoration of

---

[87] See the works of Graham Parry, Kenneth Fincham, Julian Davies and Nicholas Tyacke for details of the church policies of the 1630s.

[88] Note Laud's concern for communion tables in his instructions to Brent: appendix 9.

[89] *ODNB*: Lancelot Andrewes; Fincham, K., *Prelate as Pastor*, 1990.

[90] Fincham, K., *Prelate as Pastor*, 1990.

[91] Foster, A., 'Churchwardens' Accounts of Early Modern England and Wales: some problems to note but much to be gained', *The Parish in English Life 1400-1600*, eds. French, K., Gibbs, G., & Kumin, B., 1997, 74-93.

[92] Foster, A., 'Church Policies of the 1630s', *Conflict in Early Stuart England*, ed. Cust, R., & Hughes, A., 1989, 193-223; *Annual Accounts*, 63-149.

[93] Appendix 8; it is intriguing to note the king's view that churchwardens were actually avoiding carrying out repairs in order to obtain 'briefs' for support from taxpayers elsewhere in the country; it might be possible to check this against evidence of a rise in the number of briefs collected in the late 1620s.

[94] TNA: SP/16/188/37.

[95] TNA: SP/16/281/36.

[96] TNA: SP/16/290/113.

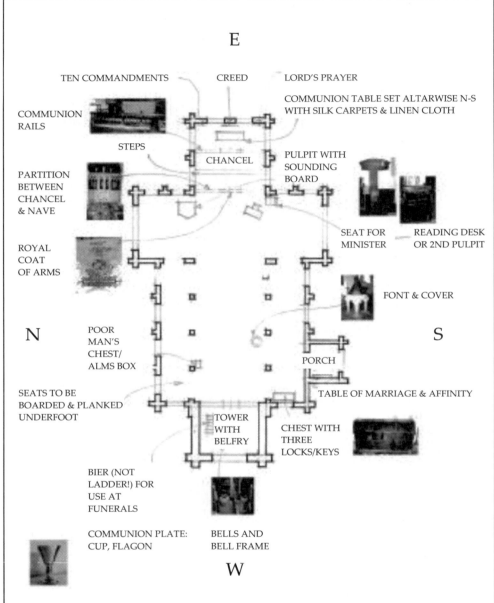

E

TEN COMMANDMENTS   CREED   LORD'S PRAYER

COMMUNION TABLE SET ALTARWISE N-S
WITH SILK CARPETS & LINEN CLOTH

COMMUNION
RAILS

STEPS

CHANCEL

PULPIT WITH
SOUNDING
BOARD

PARTITION
BETWEEN
CHANCEL
& NAVE

SEAT FOR   READING DESK
MINISTER   OR 2ND PULPIT

ROYAL
COAT
OF ARMS

FONT & COVER

N   POOR
MAN'S
CHEST/
ALMS BOX

S

PORCH

SEATS TO BE
BOARDED & PLANKED
UNDERFOOT

TABLE OF MARRIAGE & AFFINITY

TOWER
WITH
BELFRY

CHEST WITH
THREE
LOCKS/KEYS

BIER (NOT
LADDER!) FOR
USE AT
FUNERALS

COMMUNION PLATE: BELLS AND
CUP, FLAGON   BELL FRAME

W

BOOKS: REGISTERS, CANONS, BIBLE OF LATEST TRANSLATION, BOOK OF HOMILIES, BOOK OF
COMMON PRAYER, SERVICE BOOK FOR 5TH NOVEMBER
WALLS TO BE WHITEWASHED & SENTENCES OF SCRIPTURE TO BE PAINTED UP

Illustration 8: Archbishop Laud's ideal church in the 1630s?

churches and chapels. It produced documentation in a similar format to the survey of 1602, that is to say, the officials created a separate volume entirely devoted to the churches. It may well, however, be part of a much longer campaign in the diocese that probably originated with Archbishop William Laud's Metropolitical visitation of 1635. This is suggested by the fact that a separate act book supplemented the normal series of detection books for the period between October 1635 and April 1636. That act book contains classic signs of the concerns of the Archbishop.[97] Churchwardens were instructed to provide glebe terriers to show their care for church property.[98] Concern was expressed for the state of communion tables and necessary cloths. Emphasis was placed on the need to keep registers more efficiently, and also on the requirement that all churches should display a 'table of the degrees of marriage', usually positioned in the west end.[99] Such concerns were repeated in another run of cases in the summer of 1636, indicating that the authorities were maintaining their pressure on incumbents and churchwardens.[100] The church cases that appeared in the autumn of 1636 simply add to this sense of pressure being maintained. Many of the resulting church cases were still being pursued into the summer of 1637, when Bishop Montagu held his fourth visitation of the diocese.[101]

Those ultimately behind these surveys were Queen Elizabeth, James I and Charles I, together with their archbishops and the diocesan bishops. Royal authority lent bishops great support in summoning churchwardens and impropriators or their farmers alike to give an account of their churches. The people who carried out the work on the ground included a panoply of people from senior diocesan clergy and officials down to relatively humble and less well-known local clergy. Diocesan Chancellors such as Anthony Blencowe, John Drury and William Neville oversaw the work of the diocesan courts, but they also routinely gave the task of presiding over the courts to surrogates. These people were drawn from the ranks of local clergy and included Henry Blaxton, Chancellor of Chichester Cathedral, and Roger Andrewes, Chancellor and also Archdeacon of Chichester – brother of the famous Bishop Lancelot Andrewes to

[97] WSRO: Ep. I/17/26; we are grateful to Peter Wilkinson for his careful analysis of the contents of this act book and of Ep. I/17/25; this has been invaluable in our unraveling of the process described above; see appendix 10.

[98] The success of this policy may be noted from the fact that we possess glebe terriers for 1635 for 102 churches in this survey: Ep. I/88/1 typescript list; see our church list on which we have noted the survival for both 1635 and 1615. A significant number of terriers survive for these dates in the Lewes Archdeaconry.

[99] It is intriguing to speculate about this particular concern: had there been more problems with marriages in this period or are we simply dealing with officious bureaucrats? The matter might also relate to the concerns for better keeping of registers. We are grateful to Roger Davey, Trevor Cooper, and Helen Whittle for discussion of these matters. The Rt Revd Dr Michael Langrish reminded us of Archbishop Parker's interest in the 'Table of Kindred and Affinity', and noted that one of the suggested Canons of 1640 would have restricted the discretion of ordinaries on marriages. David Crankshaw has since kindly confirmed Parker's authorship of the original table. For more on this see: Cressy, D., *Birth, Marriage & Death*, 1997, 311-15.

[100] WSRO: Ep. I/17/25.

[101] WSRO: Ep. I/17/27.

whom he owed his preferment. They also included the civil lawyer Hugh Barker, who presided over the Dean's Court until 1632. Canons Residentiary of the Cathedral, such as Garrett Williamson, Richard Kitson, and William and Francis Coxe, also acted routinely as surrogates presiding over the courts that collated the reports on the churches and duly signed matters off. Another layer of officials aided them, a veritable team of notaries and registrars, led by Richard Juxon, father of William Juxon who, ended his illustrious career as Archbishop of Canterbury on the Restoration. These people were the able bureaucrats – about whom we would love to know more – who obediently drew up the papers and invariably supported the clerical establishment.[102]

What do the surveys reveal?

The transcripts provide full details of what was reported to the authorities and certain themes stand out. If Whitgift hoped that his questions about chancels might reveal neglect on the part of lay impropriators, he must have been very embarrassed. Nearly half of the impropriated livings of the archdeaconry were held by the Crown, the bishop, and the Dean and Chapter, and their livings were just as likely to be neglected and reported as those held by local gentry.[103] Even among the city of Chichester's churches we find that within the cathedral transept that formed St Peter the Great: 'the wales of the Chancell be very foule. The glase windows be very darke & much decayed. The paving is decayed and the partition is not as it ought to be.'[104] In the chancel of St Martin, 'the seates are very bad. The wales are very fowle. The windows are very darke. The commandments are decayed.'[105] The need for significant fabric repairs concerning steeples, porches, windows, roofs, floors, seats and the provision of pulpits was noted for many churches, but the reports for 1602, and relatively speedy outcome for the vast majority of churches by Easter of 1603, suggest that this survey satisfied the authorities – and may have allayed some fears – whilst also encouraging greater care in the future.[106] This would have been a satisfactory outcome for the episcopal authorities, and one that they could report dutifully to the new king.

With all of these surveys there is the tricky matter of whether we are looking at a glass half-empty or half-full. Certainly Harsnett and Laud would probably have been upset by what was uncovered, suggesting, as it did, lack of respect for churches and lack of provision of places fit for 'worship'. The reports for 1610

---

[102] Some details of all of these people and others may be found in our section on key people involved in these surveys, but it has to be admitted that much more research is needed here to bring those from the lower ranks to life.

[103] This is another matter that cries out for further research.

[104] See entries for St Peter the Great, Chichester.

[105] See entries for St Martin, Chichester.

[106] See appendix 5 and the analysis of dates by which certificates were signed off for 1602 kindly supplied by Peter Wilkinson.

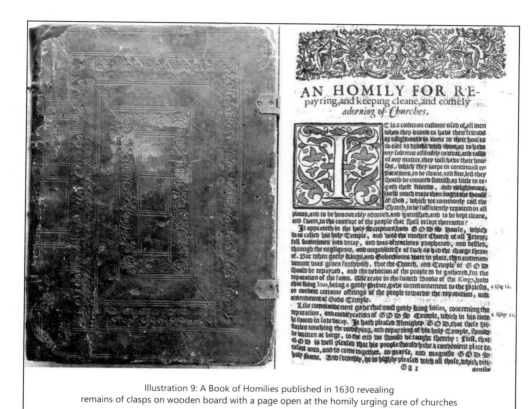

Illustration 9: A Book of Homilies published in 1630 revealing
remains of clasps on wooden board with a page open at the homily urging care of churches

cannot have made happy reading when one considers what was supposed to have been rectified by 1603. Over one third of the churches required work on their porches, while around one quarter of all the churches surveyed reported faults with their steeples, windows, general 'healing', and buttresses.[107] It could hardly inspire confidence that Binderton, for example, presented that 'our steeple is in default for want of shingle and our church windows both want glasinge and the pavement of our church is verie much broken we likewise have no pulpit and our communion cloth is verie bad and unseemly for the place'.[108] And again, it should have been a matter of some concern that at St Peter the Great in Chichester, 'the glass windowes from our parish church are much decayed which ought to be mended by the Deane and Chapter there is otherwise lacking a pulpit clothe and cushion & carpet with a lynnen cloth to cover the communion table and a table of the degrees of marriage there is likewise wanting a silver or pewter pott for the communion.'[109] An indication of

---

[107] See glossary of terms for 'healing'.
[108] See entries for Binderton.
[109] See entries for St Peter the Great, Chichester.

Harsnett's leanings may be detected in concerns raised about communion tables and fonts for around 20 churches, but that is offset by an interest also in that traditional Puritan preserve, the pulpit. What is very different from the later survey of 1636, however, is the absence of many pettifogging concerns regarding registers, books or those tables of degrees of marriage.

It is the survey of 1636 that provides most scope for statistical treatment, because it was clearly laid out in a form that appears to have been answering a list of very detailed questions. In the archdeaconry in 1636, around 40% of all churches lacked a decent Book of Common Prayer, over 30% lacked a book of Canons, while 46% lacked a Book of Homilies. Even more annoying for the likes of Montagu and Laud, 48% of the churches lacked decent pulpit furnishings, while 52% lacked decent communion table furnishings; 80% lacked a flagon and few kept adequate records of their church plate. In all, over 40% of the churches were reported for having problems with their communion tables, over a quarter for inadequate rails – the novel policy that was such a feature of the campaigns in the 1630s – while around a quarter of churches noted problems with their fonts and lack of covers.[110] Structural defects were reported in many cases, but the above statistics reveal the overall tone and direction of the 'Laudian' campaign in Sussex, largely overseen by Bishop Montagu.[111]

The authorities would have gleaned a lot of information from these surveys, but how do we measure the success with which they tackled the problems raised? They maintained pressure as we can see from the aftermath of the 1602 survey. Churchwardens and impropriators or farmers were held to account and most appear to have certified by Easter of 1603. Others were doggedly pursued through court hearings that lasted until March 1604.[112] Yet close inspection of the table relating to the provision of certificates makes somewhat sad reading: the churchwardens of 82 out of 123 churches did indeed sign off at Easter 1603 as requested when first presented back in the autumn; but repairs for only 61 chancels were also signed off by that date.[113] Worse still, at the end of this process, no certificates had been received regarding 52 chancels, or from the churchwardens of 18 churches.[114] It was clearly easier to bring churchwardens to heel than it was the impropriators or farmers of the livings.

What is just as telling, however, is that many of the churches for which repairs were duly certified appeared again with fairly substantial problems in 1610.

---

[110] Fincham & Tyacke, *Altars Restored, 2007, passim.*

[111] For an earlier analysis of this campaign see: Fletcher, A., *A County Community in Peace and War*, 1975 who unfortunately made a number of assertions about resistance in East Sussex and the dating of campaigns that simply cannot be verified owing to lack of sources.

[112] See appendices 2 and 5 for details of the campaigns.

[113] Appendix 5 kindly provided by Peter Wilkinson.

[114] *Ibid.*

There is scope for much more research here, but just a few examples serve to make the point. The church of Sidlesham was reported in 1610 to have 'windowes in parte stopped up with stones, the south outlet in decay', problems with 'the timber worke of the roofe' and 'the shingles of the steeple', likewise with their porch, while the communion table was considered to be 'undecent'. It was admittedly much worse in 1602, when the seats of the aisles were noted as being broken, the roof in decay, the pulpit needing work, the belfry floor broken, and the steeple, bells and porch needing work, but that porch (or outlet) still sounds to have been in trouble in 1610.[115] It was a similar story at Elsted, where in 1610 the church was in 'great decay in healinge, in the buttresses & wall, the wall wants coating on the south side, the communion table undecent, the church porch in decay' and 'the rafters in the north wall very rotten'. Yet in 1602, the churchwardens had also been lambasted because the church needed 'wasshinge the seats are unplancked the windowes are in defalte, it rayneth into the church through the steeple'; the roof clearly needed mending and sadly the communion table had also been found to be 'undecent'.[116] Even closer to home, under the eyes of the authorities in Chichester, problems could still go unresolved. At St Peter the Less, the minister presented his churchwardens in 1610 for failing to report that they lacked a Book of Homilies, that windows were in decay, that the font lacked paving underfoot, nor did it hold water, that they had no pulpit, and lacked a number of other items.[117] Back in 1602, the same church had needed much work on the paving, seats, walls, roof and steeple.[118]

At St Peter the Great, housed within the cathedral, the finger was pointed very clearly at the Dean and Chapter for their failure to repair windows, while they too lacked appropriate pulpit cloths, cloths for the communion table or appropriate silverware. This at least was less reprehensible that what had been reported in 1602. Then, the walls of the chancel had been condemned as 'very foule', the glass windows 'very darke & much decayed', and the paving poor; the churchwardens were required to repair numerous seats, take better care of the font, and also – something echoed alas in 1610 – the communion table. Overall, it was considered that 'the church is most fowly kept by the clarke'![119] Readers may use the entries that follow to analyse for themselves with what success the faults reported were handled.

When the picture for 1636 gets flooded with details of schemes for 'beautification' of churches, provision of better surplices, communion plate and

---

[115] See entries for Sidlesham.
[116] See entries for Elsted.
[117] Trevor Cooper has remarked on the significance of the number of pulpit complaints being registered in the survey for 1602, another matter for further research.
[118] See entries for St Peter the Less, Chichester.
[119] See entries for St Peter the Great (the Subdeanery), Chichester.

cloth, cushions for the pulpit, covers for fonts, appropriate service books and registers, it might appear as if concerns about the fabric had been largely resolved at last. Yet even here, we need to be cautious as the following case study reveals.

Words of warning as revealed by a case study of St Mary's, Slindon in the 1630s.

A case study relating to St Mary's, Slindon is informative for a number of reasons: it reveals that we should not see these surveys in isolation, clearly focused and full though they appear. Church cases, as already noted, came up in the church courts fairly routinely, albeit not usually providing the detail of the surveys of 1602 or 1636. And sadly, we should not see the surveys and any certificates of work completed as necessarily conveying an accurate picture. The surveys provide an excellent snapshot in time of the state of the churches, but they also obscure the fact of life for churchwardens that the battle to maintain churches – as today – is never-ending, and also a fairly thankless task.

A case regarding the church of St Mary's in Slindon, a small parish on the edge of the Downs, was brought to the attention of the court held for the Peculiar in All Saints, Chichester in March 1632/3, when it was reported that the 'church is at defaulte in the healing'.[120] In July of that year, this was still the case, while it was also reported that 'the wall that is the partition between the Chancell and the Church is like to fall down to the great danger of the Church and Chancell.'[121] In May 1634 the wall was still posing problems and the churchwardens were given more time to carry out appropriate repairs.[122] Excuses flew in a court sitting held in June, when the weather and other impediments were blamed for slow progress.[123] In November 1634, it was reported that the wall had almost been fully repaired, but the churchwardens were still being asked for a final certificate in January 1635 and again in that summer.[124] It was not until October 1635 that it was agreed that 'the most parte of the Church is repaired'.[125] Yet in November 1635, possibly as a result of the Metropolitical visitation, it was recorded that a glebe terrier was required – something that rings true for the majority of parishes in the archdeaconry and which had featured in a separate detection book for the archdeaconry. Worse still, however, the parish clerk could not read or write, and men had been found playing 'shovell board' on the communion table between working on the church repairs.[126]

---

[120] WSRO: Ep. IV/2/14, f.103v; to make matters worse this problem had actually been reported as far back as October 1629, f.4r.
[121] *Ibid.*, f.126v.
[122] *Ibid.*, f.151v.
[123] *Ibid.*, f.155.
[124] *Ibid.*, ff.168 & 173.
[125] *Ibid.*, f.192.
[126] *Ibid.*, f.199v.

In April 1636 the churchwardens were ordered to repair the whole church and to clear rubbish around the steeple.[127] Matters were still in hand in May, when it was reported that the church needed the Ten Commandments to be set up in the east end, repairs to the churchyard, and attention should be paid to some problems affecting the steeple.[128] Unfortunately, we possess no direct evidence of what occurred in the autumn of 1636 when the rest of the diocese was so strictly scrutinised. Yet despite this close attention throughout the 1630s, in December 1637 the churchwardens were forced to confess that 'our steeple is lately fallen downe.'[129]

This case illustrates how the authorities could harass the churchwardens, issue numerous instructions, receive any number of excuses, ratify delays – and even on receipt of a certificate that all had been remedied – still hear news of a major catastrophe not long after. So alas, many of the certificates noted in these surveys should be taken with a hefty pinch of salt!

Areas for further research.

The surveys cry out for further research, hence one reason for publication. Local historians may be able to pursue details about incumbents, impropriators and farmers.[130] The survey of 1602 allows us a very brief glimpse of the rectors, impropriators of livings and their farmers: it would be helpful to know more about them and their role in their communities, people such as Richard Snelling, who appears to have been responsible for a cluster of chancels at East Preston, Ferring and Kingston. Likewise, Thomas Haberden at East Dean, or one of the few women noted in these records, Elinor Weston at Earnley.[131] Researchers with complete lists of churchwardens might be able to track through other sources the efforts, successful or not, of those who bore the burden of raising money for the repairs of naves.[132] Architectural historians might be able to examine the material evidence of work on buttresses, steeples, towers, windows and

---

[127] *Ibid.*, f.214v.

[128] *Ibid.*, f.218.

[129] WSRO: Ep. IV/2/15, f.24v.

[130] In the process, it will be possible to correct the many errors and gaps that may be found in our list, compiled though it has been with the aid of the latest data available through CCEd.

[131] Names of impropriators or farmers of livings, where known, are given with each church. It should be remembered that where the Rector of the living was a clergyman, he will be found to have been responsible for the chancel; and this was indeed the case for over 40 of our archdeaconry churches. It should not be assumed that the impropriator of the living was necessarily the patron of the living, for the advowson to present might have been sold or given away, a situation famous in the novels of Jane Austen and Anthony Trollope.

[132] Compilation of lists of the humble churchwardens would be invaluable in helping us to come to understand more clearly how they worked in the community, the families and social strata from which they were drawn, their frequency of service – and even in some cases, where some might have been 'Church Papists' keeping an eye on *their* churches and family monuments.

porches.[133] Many historians today have embraced interest in 'material culture' – the evidence yielded by artefacts from the period – and Joan Barham found that valuable silverware shedding great light on churches in this period has found its way into the Cathedral Treasury.[134] The material poses special problems regarding trends in some areas: what was happening to church porches for example, or pulpits – and how many of those may we now confidently describe as being 'Jacobean'. Specialists have already invested much time and energy in discovering Caroline 'altars' and altar rails, while others have noted those that were lost in the iconoclasm of the British Civil Wars.[135] Others with an interest in the continuing support for Roman Catholicism in the south might note the presence of notable Catholic patrons like Viscount Montague of Midhurst or the Kempes of Slindon, ponder on their network of associates acting as farmers, and speculate on the implications of their continued involvement in the maintenance of *their* parish churches.[136]

What did the repairs required for these churches cost and how was money raised? In the case of chancels, it was down to the impropriator (clerical or lay) or his farmer to raise the funds and carry out work. For the body of the church, churchwardens had recourse to 'landscots' to raise taxes on all households or those that held land, assuming that repairs could not be covered under normal income and expenditure.[137] Valerie Hitchman has provided a valuable index of material goods and services likely to be involved and their costs during this period.[138] We possess some clues for Sussex in surviving churchwardens' accounts. Billingshurst, for example, spent over £29 in 1611 on repairs to the steeple and bells, when expenditure for earlier years had averaged £2 per annum. A further £16 was spent on bells in 1615. In 1635, £19 was spent on whitening, trimming and repairing, while £19 was also spent in 1636, fifty shillings of which was the cost of railing the Communion Table.[139] In Horsham in 1611, £25 was spent of which £16 was raised by landscot. £10 was spent on shingles for the steeple in 1615. These accounts provide evidence of support for

---

[133] This was a feature of Joan Barham's MPhil thesis of 2010, one product of which was the creation of a gazetteer of Sussex churches compiled on the basis of a wide range of sources including architectural evidence: see the bibliography.

[134] Barham thesis noted above; Michael Moriarty curates the Treasury at Chichester Cathedral and has kindly informed us of at least seven communion cups held there which may be dated to the 1630s: Bepton, Billingshurst, Ferring, Funtington, Keymer, Rye and Woolbeding.

[135] Fincham & Tyacke, *Altars Restored*, 2007; Cooper, T., ed., *The Journal of William Dowsing*, 2001.

[136] For more on the continued importance of Roman Catholics in the country see: Shiels, W., 'Getting on' and 'getting along' in parish and town: Catholics and their neighbours in England', in *Catholic Communities in Protestant States: Britain and the Netherlands, c.1570-1720*, ed. Kaplan, B., et al, 2009, 67-83; Shagan, E., ed., *Catholics and the Protestant Nation*, 2005; and the monumental study for Sussex: Questier, M., *Catholicism and Community in Early Modern England*, 2006.

[137] For details of what was available to churchwardens see the articles contained in Hitchman, V., and Foster, A., eds, *Views from the Parish*, 2015.

[138] Hitchman, V., 'Balancing the Parish Accounts', in *Views from the Parish, op.cit.*, 15-45.

[139] WSRO: PAR 21/9/1, Billingshurst accounts 1520-1639.

the campaign to raise money for St Paul's, to which the parish gave 11s 2d in 1633, and a further 15s 6d in 1635. A new bell from the notable Sussex foundry of Brian Eldridge cost money in 1633, while much of the £29 19s 8d spent in 1636 was for work around the communion table.[140]

The churchwardens' accounts that survive for the period corroborate the interest being shown in the parish churches in the early seventeenth century. Concerns perhaps first sparked in 1602 evidently led to results and sustained efforts to restore churches; communities were mobilised. How willingly is another matter, and also with what degree of success. While much of the work under James I might have been carried out fairly willingly, there is evidence of controversy when the changes required under Charles I seemed to carry doctrinal overtones.[141] The changes may not have been as expensive as earlier work, but they could rankle with those more Puritanically and evangelically minded. Increasing numbers of people refusing to pay their rates is, however, one backhanded compliment to the success of these campaigns.[142]

There is always the question of the reliability of these surveys. It should be noted that the 'system' was entirely dependent upon the oaths of the churchwardens, self-reporting on oath. Rarely do we hear of visits by officials in the follow-up to Sussex cases, although we know that such visits were a feature of the success of the campaigns in the north.[143] Charles I clearly had a low view of the words of churchwardens as his Proclamation of 1629 reveals.[144] There would also have been considerable problems in tracking impropriators and farmers to pay their fair share for the upkeep of the chancels – as revealed in appendix 5 – without which, the rest of the fabric was also endangered.

Conclusions

The Slindon case study illustrates just how much more needs to be done through micro-histories to uncover the full story of what was happening in our churches in the early seventeenth century. The surveys that we publish here offer 'snapshots' that need to be followed up by use of a wide variety of records and architectural fieldwork. The surveys open up enquiries into many spheres, for we need to learn much more about the clergy who held these livings and the churchwardens who served their communities. Such enquiries lead on to matters of wider ecclesiastical policy concerning the attitudes and theological inclinations of the bishops and senior clergy of this diocese, and the degree of

---

[140] WSRO: PAR 106/9/1, Horsham accounts 1610-1770; see Hughes thesis noted in the bibliography.
[141] Foster, 'Churchwardens' accounts'; MacCulloch, 'Myth of the Reformation'.
[142] Foster, 'Church Policies'.
[143] Foster, 'Church Policies'.
[144] Appendix 8.

control they exercised over the region. The problem of enforcement of policies and repairs poses questions about the financial ability of the communities to pay. In an effort to provide some clues on that score, details of the rough figures of the value of each living have been provided drawn from the out-of-date, but still used, measure of the time, the King's Book.[145] Although these figures were scarcely inflation proof, they do afford a comparative view of the parishes in the diocese and the relationship between wealthier and poorer livings. Those churches where the incumbents were rectors have also been indicated on the church list, as their income would certainly have mattered if they were to fulfil their obligations to take care of the chancels.

First and foremost, these surveys reveal the continuing struggle to identify and establish what a Protestant church should look like in post-Reformation England and Wales. And most churches clearly did not look in terribly good condition in 1602. The surveys highlight the significance of the Canons of 1604 in raising and clarifying the benchmark for all concerned. They shed light on the struggles in practice of those in authority – bishops and archdeacons responsible for raising standards – their parochial clergy, hard-pressed churchwardens, taxed congregations, and non clerical impropriators who were accountable for the state of so many chancels. Finally, what is revealed in 1636 is the extent to which there was an ideological struggle going on with one wing of the church urging concern for sacramental worship over preaching, and doing so in a fairly heavy handed fashion, something which gave offence to many and was a factor in the origins of the British Civil Wars.

Many excellent research projects may be prompted by the contents of this volume, but our purpose has been served in making the text available, providing it with lavish illustrations, and hopefully making it serviceable for the needs of a wide range of readers. We hope that this volume will stimulate research, become a useful guide for those who enjoy visiting ancient churches, and serve as a reliable reference work for those interested in this topic, period and region.[146]

---

[145] *Thesaurus Rerum Ecclesiasticarum being an Account of the Valuations of all the Ecclesiastical Benefices in the several Dioceses of England and Wales*, Ecton, J., ed., 3rd edition, 1763, 52-67; these figures have been rounded to the nearest pound.
[146] We respectfully urge its use alongside the indispensible: Nairn, I., & Pevsner, N., eds., *Sussex, The Buildings of England*, 1965.

BIBLIOGRAPHY

Manuscripts: West Sussex Record Office:
Manuscripts from which transcripts were drawn for this volume:

Ep. I/26/1	1602-3 Church surveys – Chichester Archdeaconry (34ff)
Ep. I/26/2	1636 Church surveys – Chichester Archdeaconry (37ff)
Ep. III/6/Box 407/folder 3/25	
	Church surveys for Dean of Chichester's Peculiar jurisdiction – undated, but form suggests 1602/3 (2ff)
Ep. IV/2/8	Church surveys located within detection book for the Archbishop of Canterbury's Peculiar of Pagham & Tarring 1602/3 (ff21r-24r)
Ep. I/17/13	Church surveys located within detection court book of the Archdeaconry of Chichester for the autumn of 1610 (ff84-114)

Manuscripts consulted for context:

Ep.I/17/10	detection book Chi. Archdeaconry 1600-1603 (247ff)
Ep. I/17/11	detection book Chi. Archdeaconry 1603-1606 (273ff)
Ep. I/17/25	detection book Chi. Archdeaconry 1633-1637 (375ff)
Ep. I/17/26	detection book Chi. Archdeaconry 1635-1636 (38ff)
Ep. I/17/27	detection book Chi. Archdeaconry 1637-1641 (371ff)
Ep. I/18/26	liber cleri for Visitation of Archbishop Bancroft, 1605 (18ff)
Ep. I/18/27	liber cleri for Primary Visitation of Bishop Andrewes, 1606 (26ff)
Ep. I/18/30	liber cleri for Primary Visitation of Bishop Harsnett, 1610 (27ff)
Ep. I/18/32	liber cleri for Metro. Visitation of Archbishop Abbot, 1615 (25ff)
Ep. I/22/1	churchwardens' loose presentments
Ep. I/25/1-3	church terriers for Chi. Archdeaconry - see calendar Ep I/88/1
Ep. IV/2/9	detection book for Pagham & Tarring Peculiar 1609-14 (84ff)
Ep. IV/2/10	detection book for Pagham & Tarring Peculiar 1614-15 (16ff)
Ep. IV/2/11	detection book for Pagham & Tarring Peculiar 1615-16 (31ff)
Ep. IV/2/14	detection book for Pagham & Tarring Peculiar 1629-36 (228ff)
Ep. III/4/6	detection book for Dean of Chichester's Peculiar 1601-05 (73ff)
Ep. III/4/8	detection book for Dean of Chichester's Peculiar 1610-14 (93ff)
Ep. III/4/12	detection book for Dean of Chichester's Peculiar 1629-37 (274ff)
Ep. III/7/1-9	churchwardens' loose presentments for Dean's Peculiar

Material checked for the Archdeaconry of Lewes:

Ep. II/9/9   detection book 1600-1605 (278ff)
Ep. II/9/11   detecton book 1606-1610 (281ff)
Ep. II/9/12   detection book 1610-1613 (157ff)
Ep. II/9/22   detection book April-December 1635 (63ff)
Ep. II/9/23   detection book Oct. 1636-1639 (136ff)
Ep. II/10/1   libri cleri 1600-1607 (84ff)
Ep. II/10/3   libri cleri 1626-1641 (130ff)
Ep. II/15/1   register of presentments 1637-1639
Ep. II/17   Church terriers survive in large numbers for 1615-16, 1635-36

Churchwardens' Accounts survive for the following West Sussex parishes:

PAR 11/9/1   Ashurst 1522-1630
PAR 21/9/1   Billingshurst 1520-1639
PAR 37/30   St Andrew, Chichester 1616-50
PAR 48/9/1   West Chiltington 1613-1705
PAR 98/12/1   South Harting 1601-1803
PAR 106/9/1   Horsham 1610-1770
PAR 160/12/1   Rudgwick 1579-1835

WSRO Accession 9822: the collection of photographs commissioned by Archdeacon John Walker in 1879

Evidence about clergy & patrons has been collated from several sources:

CCEd   The clergy of the Church of England database, 1540-1835,
                www.theclergydatabase.org.uk
G. Hennessy, *Chichester Diocese Clergy Lists*, 1900
W.D. Peckham, Clergy Lists held at WSRO

Printed Primary and Secondary Material

Addleshaw, E. & Etchells, F., *The Architectural Setting of Anglican Worship*, 1948
Babbage, S., *Puritanism and Richard Bancroft*, 1962
Bray, G., ed., *The Anglican Canons 1529-1947*, COERS, 6, 1998
Brinkworth, E., 'The Laudian Church in Buckinghamshire', *University of Birmingham Historical Journal*, V, 1955, 31-59
Burgess, C., 'Pre-Reformation Churchwardens' Accounts and Parish Government: Lessons from London and Bristol', *English Historical Review*, 117, 2002, 306-32

Chapman, C.R., *Ecclesiastical courts, their officials and their records*, 1992

Chatfield, M., ed., *Churches the Victorians Forgot*, 1989

Collinson, P., 'The Elizabethan Church and the New Religion', in *The Reign of Elizabeth I*, ed. Haigh, C., 1984, 169-194

Cooper, T., ed., *The Journal of William Dowsing Iconoclasm in East Anglia during th English Civil War*, 2001

Cooper, T. & Brown, S., eds., *Pews, Benches and Chairs: Church Seating in English Parish Churches from the Fourteenth Century to the Present*, Ecclesiological Society, 2011

Cox, J. C. & Harvey, A., *English Church Furniture*, 1907

Cox, J.C., *English Church Fittings, Furniture and Accessories*, 1923

Cressy, D., *Birth, Marriage & Death Ritual, Religion, and the Life-Cycle in Tudor and Stuart England*, 1997

Davies, J., *The Caroline Captivity of the Church: Charles I and the Remoulding of Anglicanism*, 1992

Delderfield, E., *Church Furniture*, 1966

Diocese of Chichester: A Catalogue of the Records of the Bishop, Archdeacons and Former Exempt Jurisdictions, compiled by Steer, F. & Kirby, I., WSCC, 1966

Duffy, E., *The Voices of Morebath. Reformation and Rebellion in an English Village*, 2001

Duffy, E., *The Stripping of the Altars. Traditional Religion in England c.1400-c.1580*, 1992

Dyer, A. & Palliser, D., eds., *The Diocesan Population Returns for 1563 and 1603*, 2005

Elton, G., *England 1200-1640: The Sources of History*, 1969

The English Parish Church Through the Centuries, Interactive CD ROM, ed. Dyas, D., Christianity & Culture project, University of York, 2010

Farrant, J. ed., *Sussex Depicted Views and Descriptions 1600-1800*, SRS, 85, 2001

Fincham, K., *Prelate as Pastor The Episcopate of James I*, 1990

Fincham, K., ed., *Visitation Articles and Injunctions of the Early Stuart Church. Volume I*, COERS, 1, 1994

Fincham, K. ed., *Visitation Articles and Injunctions of the Early Stuart Church Volume II*, COERS, 5, 1998

Fincham, K. & Tyacke, N., *Altars Restored The Changing Face of English Religious Worship, 1547-c.1700*, 2007

Fincham, K., ed., 'Annual accounts of the Church of England, 1632-1639', in *From the Reformation to the permissive society*, ed. Barber, M., Taylor, S., and Sewell, G., COERS, 18, 2010, 63-149

Fletcher, A., *A County Community in Peace and War: Sussex 1600-1660*, 1975

Foster, A., 'Church Policies of the 1630s', *Conflict in Early Stuart England*, eds., Cust, R., & Hughes, A., 1989, 193-223

Foster, A., 'Chichester Diocese in the Seventeenth Century', *SAC*, 123, 1985, pp. 187-194

Foster, A., 'Churchwardens' Accounts of Early Modern England and Wales: some problems to note but much to be gained', *The Parish in English Life 1400-1600*, eds., K. French, G. Gibbs & B. Kumin, MUP, 1997, pp.74-93

Foster, A., 'Bishops of Chichester 1503-1709', in *Chichester – The Palace and its Bishops*, ed. Foster, P, & Moriarty, R., Otter Memorial Paper, 27, 2011, 132-9

Foster, A., 'The Episcopal Palace and residences of the Bishops of Chichester 1500-1700', in *Chichester – The Palace and its Bishops* cited above, 167-74

Foster, A., et al, *Aspects of the Religious History of Slindon since the Reformation*, Slindon Local History Group, 2013

Foster, A., 'Bishops, Church, and State, c.1530-1646' in *The Oxford History of Anglicanism, Volume I*, ed. Milton, A., 2017, 84-102

Foster, C.W., ed., *The State of the Church, Vol I, Lincoln Record Society*, 23, 1926, pp. 219-36 covers returns made in 1602 for the archdeaconries of Lincoln and Stowe (some 635 churches)

Ford, W.K., ed., *Chichester Diocesan Surveys 1686 and 1724*, SRS, 78, 1994

Gaimster, D. & Gilchrist, R., eds., *The Archaeology of Reformation 1480-1580*, 2003

Gibbs, R., 'The State of Buckinghamshire Parish Churches in the 16th and 17th centuries', *Records of Buckinghamshire*, 6, 1887, 150-67, 245-58

Goring, J., 'The Reformation of the Ministry in Elizabethan Sussex', *Journal of Ecclesiastical History*, 34, 1983, 345-366

Guinn-Chipman, S., *Religious Space in Reformation England*, 2013

Haigh, C., 'The Taming of the Reformation: Preachers, Pastors and Parishioners in Elizabethan and Early Stuart England', *History*, 85, 2000, 572-88

Heal, F., *Of Prelates and Princes A Study of the Economic and Social Position of the Tudor Episcopate*, 1980

Hill, C., *Economic Problems of the Church*, 1956

Hitchman, V., *Omnia bene or Ruinosa. The Condition of the Parish Churches in and around London and Westminster c.1603-1677*, 2009

Hitchman, V., & Foster, A., eds., *Views from the Parish Churchwardens' Accounts c.1500-c.1800*, 2015

Hobbs, M., ed., *Chichester Cathedral. An Historical Survey*, 1994

Hughes, A., ed., *Sussex Clergy Inventories 1600-1750*, SRS, 91, 2009

Johnstone, H., ed., *Churchwardens' Presentments (17th Century) Part I. Archdeaconry of Chichester*, SRS, 49, 1949

Johnstone, H., ed., *Churchwardens' Presentments (17th Century) Part II. Archdeaconry of Lewes*, SRS, 50, 1950

Kaufman, L., 'Ecclesiastical Improvements, Lay Impropriations, and the Building of a Post-Reformation church in England, 1560-1600', *Historical Journal*, 2015, 1-23

Kumin, B., *The Shaping of a Community: The Rise and Reformation of the English Parish c.1400-1560*, 1996

Lake, P., 'The Laudian Style: Order, Uniformity and the Pursuit of the Beauty of Holiness in the 1630s' in *The Early Stuart Church*, ed. Fincham, K., 1993, 161-185.

Laud, W., *The History of the Troubles and Tryal of …William Laud*, 1695.

Levack, B., *The Civil Lawyers in England, 1603-41*, 1973

Lewycky, N. & Morton, A., *Getting Along? Religious Identities and Confessional Relations in Early Modern England: Essays in Honour of Professor W.J. Sheils*, 2012

MacCulloch, D., 'The Myth of the English Reformation', *Journal of British Studies*, 30, 1991, 1-19

Marchant, R., 'The Restoration of Nottinghamshire Churches, 1635-40', *Transactions of the Thoroton Society*, LXV, 1961, pp.58-93

Marchant, R., *The Church under the Law: Justice, Administration and Discipline in the Diocese of York*, 1969

Marsh, C., 'Order and Place in England, 1580-1640: The View from the Pew', *Journal of British Studies*, 44, 2005, 3-26

Marsh, C., Sacred Space in England, 1560-1640: The View from the Pew', *Journal of Ecclesiastical History*, 53,2, 2002, 286-311

Mears, N. & Ryrie, A., eds., *Worship and the Parish Church in Early Modern England*, 2013

Merritt, J., 'Puritans, Laudians, and the Phenomenon of Church-Building in Jacobean London, *Historical Journal*, 41, 1998,

Merritt, J., 'The Cradle of Laudianism? Westminster Abbey, 1558-1630', *Journal of Ecclesiastical History*, 52,4, 2001, 623-46

Merritt, J., 'The social context of the parish church in early modern Westminster', *Urban History Yearbook*, 1991, 20-31

Merritt, J., 'Religion and the English Parish', in *The Oxford History of Anglicanism, Volume* I, ed. Milton, A., 2017, 122-147

Mole, N., 'Church-Building and Popular Piety in Early Seventeenth Century Exeter', *Southern History*, 25, 2003, 8-38

Nairn, I. & Pevsner, N., eds.,*Sussex, The Buildings of England*, 1965.

Outhwaite, R.B., *The rise and fall of the English ecclesiastical courts, 1500-1860*, 2006

O'Day, R., & Heal, F., eds., *Princes & Paupers in the English Church 1500-1800*, 1981

Parry, G., *Glory, Laud and Honour: The Arts of the Anglican Counter-Reformation*, 2006

Peckham, W.D., *The Acts of the Dean and Chapter of the Cathedral Church of Chichester 1545-1642, SRS,* 58, 1959

Purvis, Canon J.S., *The Condition of Yorkshire Church Fabrics 1300-1800,* Borthwick Institute of Historical Research, St. Anthony's Hall Publications, 14, 1958

Questier, M., *Catholicism and Community in Early Modern England,* 2006

Renshaw, W.C., ed., *Ecclesiastical Returns for 81 Parishes in East Sussex, made in 1603, SRS,* IV, 1905, 3-17

Shagan, E., ed., *Catholics and the 'Protestant Nation',* 2005

Sheils, W., 'Catholics and their Neighbours in a Rural Community: Egton Chapelry 1590-1780', *Northern History,* 34, 1998, 109-133

Sheils, W., ''Getting on' and 'getting along' in parish and town: Catholics and their neighbours in England', in *Catholic Communities in Protestant States: Britain and the Netherlands, c1570-1720,* ed. Kaplan, B., et al, 2009, 67-83

Smith, V. *Sussex Churches The Sharpe Collection of Watercolours and Drawings 1797 - 1809 mainly by Henry Petrie F.S.A.* (Sussex Archaeological Society 1979)

Strype, J., *The Life and Acts of...John Whitgift DD.,* 1718.

Thesaurus Rerum Ecclesiasticarum being an Account of the Valuations of all the Ecclesiastical Benefices in the several Dioceses of England and Wales, Ecton, J., ed., 3rd edition, 1763

Usher, B., *William Cecil and Episcopacy, 1559-1577,* 2003

Usher, R., *The Reconstruction of the English Church,* II vols., 1910

Walsham, A., 'The Parochial roots of Laudianism revisited: Catholics, Anti-Calvinists, and 'Parish Anglicans' in Early Stuart England,' *Journal of Ecclesiastical History,* 49 (4), 620-651

Whiteman, K & J., *Ancient Churches of Sussex* (Roedale Books 1994)

Whiting, R., *The Reformation of the English Parish Church,* 2010

Willis, J., *The Reformation of the Decalogue: Religious Identity and the Ten Commandments in England, c.1485-1580,* 2017

Wilkinson, P., 'Diocesan Business: The Bishop's Work and the Bishop's Records', in *Chichester – The Palace and its Bishops,* ed. Foster, P. & Moriarty, R., Otter Memorial Papers, 27, 2011, 209-15

Wilkinson, P., ed. *Chichester Archdeaconry Depositions 1603-1608, SRS,* 97, 2017

Yates, N. *Buildings, Faith, and Worship,* 1991

Yule, G., 'James VI and I: furnishing the churches in his two kingdoms', *Religion, Culture and Society in Early Modern Britain,* ed. Fletcher, A. & Roberts, P., 1994, 182-208

Theses:

Barham, J., 'The Impact of the Reformation on the fabric and furnishings of
    Sussex churches, c.1540-1640', (Unpublished MPhil thesis, University
    of Southampton, 2010)
Hughes, A., 'An examination of the Horsham Churchwardens' Accounts, 1610-
    1642', (Unpublished MA thesis, University of Sussex, 1983)
Reeks, J., 'Parish Religion in Somerset 1625-1662 with Particular Reference to
    the Churchwardens', (Unpublished PhD thesis, University of Bristol,
    2014)
Vickers, N., 'Changes in 17th Century Yorkshire Parish Church Furniture and
    Fittings as a result of religious upheavals 1603-1660', (Unpublished
    MPhil thesis, University of Hull, 1992)

Websites:

www.theclergydatabase.org.uk
Oxford Dictionary of National Biography: www.ODNB
sussexparishchurches.org
leweshistory.org.uk

Visitation Articles:

*Articles ministered by the Reverend Father in God, Thomas [Bickley], by the grace of
God Bishop of Chichester, to the churchwardens throughout the whole diocese of
Chichester at the visitation begun there the 14 September 1586, and to be inquired of
quarterly within the said diocese, 1586*

*Articles ministered by the Reverend Father in God, Anthony [Watson] by the grace of
God Bishop of Chichester to the Churchwardens throughout the whole Diocese of
Chichester at the visitation begun there the 6 of September 1600, and to be enquired of
quarterly within the saide Diocesse, 1600*

*Articles to be enquired of in the ordinary Visitation of the worshipfull Mr Lawrence
Pay, Archdeacon of Chichester, 1635*

EDITORIAL POLICY AND NOTES ON ILLUSTRATIONS

In keeping with common record society practice, and in the interest of providing as clear a text as possible for the reader to quote with confidence, it has been decided to maintain the spelling and form of material as found in the documents. Common abbreviations found in secretary hand have been extended; use of capitals is as erratic as in the original.

In order to enhance readability, however, the entries for 1602 have been spaced differently from the compact, dense, unpunctuated entries as found. Readers may see what the editors have had to cope with by reference to Illustrations 1-4 with pictures of the original documents for each survey. We heartily endorse the classic archivists' tip to read such material aloud in order to gain a better sense of meaning and enjoyment of the dialect.

Again by common convention, square brackets [ ] have been employed on the various occasions when the editors have been defeated by the text, or words are missing, and we have supplied an educated guess!

On some occasions, chiefly in relation to material on the 1630s, crossings out have been indicated. It is difficult to know how to interpret these: were they where items had been dealt with at some later stage, or more prosaically, occasions on which the scribes noted that they had made an error and replicated entries or placed them incorrectly? This is certainly obvious for some of the crossings out detected for 1602, when material was recorded against the chancel and then placed below as really appertaining to the nave.

Dates have been modernised and the year is deemed to start on 1 January.

The text included is simply that which describes the condition of the churches; it does not include any of the court material, written in heavily abbreviated and technical Latin, usually referring matters to be reported at a later sitting of the church courts. As the survey for 1602 includes fairly full details of later court appearances, it has been possible to produce a table, reproduced in appendix 5, which records if and when certificates were given for the church repairs. As the later surveys reveal, however, these should not be treated as gospel.

It is possible to pursue many cases through the court proceedings, whether recorded with the survey, as in the case of 1602, through indicative court dates as with 1636, or within the main run of detection books, as with 1610. Such research will reveal the difficulties the authorities had in getting cases signed off, or to put it another way, the difficulties that beset hard-pressed churchwardens as they laboured to maintain their churches.

Where possible, photographs of the parish church have been provided for each place, derived from three main sources: first, the Sharpe Collection of watercolours and line drawings of Henry Petrie made between 1797 and 1809, held at Michelham Priory, Upper Dicker, Hailsham, the property of the Sussex Archaeological Society. Second, photographs drawn from the collection compiled for Archdeacon Walker's visitation of 1879, some 168 images in all. This is a remarkable collection considering that these photographs were taken only 30 years or so after Fox Talbot's pioneering work on photography. And finally, photographs have been derived from the collection made by Joan Barham, when she and her husband Jon surveyed all the churches of the diocese in connection with her MPhil thesis completed in 2010; a small number of churches have been photographed since 2010, specially for this volume. We are grateful to all who gave their permission for the reproduction or production of these images.

Henry Petrie (1768-1842) was an artist and antiquarian of distinction who became a Fellow of the Society of Antiquaries, and Keeper of the Records of the Tower of London in 1819. He conducted an impressive survey of English churches in the southern counties around 1800, and produced a magnificent collection of line drawings and watercolours that passed to his sister Clarissa and her husband the Reverend John Sharpe on his death. By a variety of strokes of good fortune this collection eventually came into the care of the Sussex Archaeological Society. Thanks largely to the efforts of Dr Sue Berry, also of SRS, this collection may now be accessed on-line through leweshistory.org.uk.

Archdeacon John Walker MA had only just been appointed Archdeacon of Chichester in 1879 when he commissioned a series of photographs, taken by numerous photographers, of the churches in his archdeaconry. This was a pioneering step, given that photography was still in its relative infancy, and an idea that was complied with no doubt to please the new archdeacon. Archdeacon Walker died in 1887, leaving us this very interesting legacy.

While the bulk of the photographs produced for each church are of exteriors, a selection of colour photographs has been supplied largely of interior fixtures and fittings, including examples of church plate largely to be found in the Treasury of Chichester Cathedral. These have all come from Joan Barham's collection. We are grateful to Michael Moriarty for assisting our enquiries with regard to the church plate held by the Cathedral, which is under his excellent care.

None of these collections has a complete set of images of all the buildings surveyed and included in this volume. We have included copies of all the relevant Petrie images now available. In the Walker collection, a number of buildings are not included, or are represented only by photographs of interiors.

We have not included modern photographs of churches that have been substantially restored or rebuilt by the Victorians, such as Duncton, Fernhurst, Littlehampton, Hunston, Northchapel, Slinfold and Selsey; meanwhile, the original churches of Chilgrove, Goring, Lordington, Treyford, Warningcamp, Durrington, Heene and Kingston have long since disintegrated: Middleton is one of the county's churches lost to the sea, with the usual local legends of the bells still being heard to toll on stormy nights. Nevertheless, we believe that this volume includes the most complete possible collection of images spanning the period concerned.

Names of incumbents have been derived from a mixture of church board listings, the list compiled by Hennessy, cross-checked with the Clergy of the Church of England Database and Peckham lists held at WSRO. No details of educational qualifications have been given here, as they were not always recorded, but they may of course be pursued by reference to the standard *Alumni* volumes produced for Oxford and Cambridge.

Details of patrons and impropriators should be treated with care. CCEd and VCH yield a lot of valuable information here, but possibly the most reliable names occur where the living was held in advowson or impropriation by the Crown, Oxbridge colleges or ecclesiastical bodies. Livings held by laymen may have changed hands more frequently. Details about either clergymen or impropriators appear most fully in the 1602 survey, much less in the later surveys. Work on supplying these details largely supplements that provided in the original documentation, and is offered here because it may provide helpful detail for researchers to pursue.

In a similar effort to assist those wishing to carry our further research, we have indicated where livings were 'rectories' and so held largely by clergymen who were responsible for their chancels. We have also indicated their crude value as derived from the *King's Book*, rounded to the nearest pound, bearing in mind that this figure was first calculated in the reign of Henry VIII, and was thus well out of date by the early seventeenth century. It continued to be used long after, however, as may be seen from the returns of the visitation in 1724, and it does at least give some indication of relative values of livings across the diocese, and together with material gleaned from glebe terriers, might indicate the relative ability of incumbents to raise funds for chancel repairs.

A glossary of terms has been added to clarify technical or archaic usages.

ABBREVIATIONS

'Annual Accounts'	'Annual Accounts of the the Church of England, 1632-1639', ed. Fincham, K., in *From Reformation to the permissive society*, ed. Barber, M., Taylor, S., & Sewell, G., COERS, XVIII, 2010, 63-149
CCEd	Clergy of the Church of England Database
COERS	Church of England Record Society
Diocese of Chichester Catalogue	*Diocese of Chichester: A Catalogue of the Records of the Bishop, Archdeacons and Former Exempt Jurisdictions*, compiled by Francis Steer and Isabel Kirby, WSCC, 1966
Foster, 'Churchwardens' Accounts'	Foster, A., 'Churchwardens' Accounts of Early Modern England and Wales: some problems to note but much to be gained', *The Parish in English Life 1400-1600*, eds., French, K., Gibbs, G., & Kumin, B., 1997, 74-93
Foster, 'Church Policies'	Foster, A., 'Church Policies of the 1630s', *Conflict in Early Stuart England*, eds., Cust, R., & Hughes, A., 1989, 193-223
Foster, Chichester Diocese	Foster, A., 'Chichester Diocese in the Seventeenth Century', *SAC*, 123, 1985, 187-194
ODNB	Oxford Dictionary of National Biography
SAC	Sussex Archaeological Collections
SRS	Sussex Record Society
TNA	The National Archives
VCH	Victoria County History
WSRO	West Sussex Record Office

GLOSSARY OF TERMS

All Saints' Day   1 November.

All Souls' Day   2 November.

Alley   an aisle in the sense of a passageway rather than in the sense of an area of the church divided by pillars from the central section.

Articles   sets of questions circulated to clergy and churchwardens in advance of a visitation by either an archbishop, a bishop, or an archdeacon; in some parts of the country articles of enquiry might also be issued by diocesan chancellors or, at a much lower level, rural deans.

Advowson   right to grant a living to a clergyman – usually held by the impropriator of the living, but the right to present the living (the advowson) could be sold or given away by 'turn' by the impropriator, thus giving someone else the right to present.

Appropriation/ impropriation   a term used to denote where the chief financial value of a living was not entirely in the hands of the incumbent clergyman, but was held by a corporate body such as a college or Dean and Chapter, a bishop or other senior clergymen, the Crown, but more commonly, by a prominent layperson. The Dissolution of the Monasteries witnessed large numbers of livings passing into lay hands, and these people duly received the 'Rectorial' or great tithes and assumed, in turn, responsibility for the upkeep of the chancel. Proportions varied across dioceses, but it was estimated by contemporaries that nearly half of all the livings in the country were impropriated. Puritan petitioners estimated in 1603 that 108 livings were impropriated, out of what they said were 300 churches in Sussex.

Archdeacon   senior clergyman appointed by a bishop to assist in running a diocese, by taking subordinate responsibility for oversight of the work of clergy, churchwardens and others within a particular area; this carried the right to hold visitations of that area annually and included inspection of churches (see Canon 86); archdeacons were commonly seen as 'the eyes of the bishop'.

Archdeaconry administrative sub-division of a diocese made up or several rural deaneries supervised by an Archdeacon.

Arminian technically a follower of the teachings of the Dutch theologian Jacobus Arminius, who at Leyden in the 1590s questioned key Calvinist tenets of predestination; such views entered Cambridge debates in the 1590s and may have influenced Lancelot Andrewes and John Overall, who added a sacramental dimension to English Arminianism, downplaying preaching, and stressing order and ceremony in worship, ideas pursued in practice by members of the 'Durham House group', and again under Archbishop Laud in the 1630s, hence also the term 'Laudian' is often used to describe this movement, a tradition picked up again in the nineteenth century by the Oxford Movement.

Baldrick the leather-lined metal strap from which a bell clapper hung.

Beautification a term for painting or whitewashing (usually with lime) a church interior which could also include provision of 'sentences of scripture' with some decoration.

Belfry that part of a tower or other structure in which bells were hung.

Benefice an ecclesiastical living.

Bible of the latest translation or a Great Bible for the use of parishioners; a desk was often built to carry such bibles which might be chained (Canon 80).

Bier moveable stand or trolley for carrying a corpse.

Book of Canons required for the use of the churchwardens and minister.

Book of Homilies required for regular use after the mid sixteenth century; these were 'sermons' authorised for use by ministers – notably non preachers and the less well educated – and covered topics such as obedience to parents, the sovereign, and good conduct in life (Canon 80).

Book of Common Prayer required by Canon 80 and laid out the prescribed liturgy for use in church services.

Book of special prayers

for example, prayers for the king's delivery 5 November.

Buttress

external support for a wall, consisting of a brick or masonry mass projecting from or built against a wall; frequently found necessary for church towers or steeples.

Canons

ecclesiastical laws established by Convocation; the Thirty-Nine Articles of 1563 (ratified by Parliament in 1571) formed the basis of the Elizabethan Church of England, and were greatly enlarged and codified by the 141 Canons agreed in 1604.

Carpet

covering of velvet, silk or buckram.

Chancel

the east end of a church, often a distinct space, where the pre-Reformation altar had stood; the communion table often stood here, though in some churches it might be moved into the body of the church for the communion service; the responsibility for maintenance and repair of the chancel rested with the Rector of the living, the person or institution to whom the 'great tithes' were paid.

Chancellor

the senior lawyer of the diocese, often also called a Vicar-General or Official Principal, who presided over the diocesan courts and adminstration – a 'Sir Humphrey' of his day.

Chest with three locks

required to keep money, registers, accounts, inventories – three locks gave security – one for the minister and one each for the churchwardens.

Church Ales

traditional occasions for parish festivities designed to raise funds; might be held on the feast date of the saint to whom the church was dedicated.

Church Rate

a local tax levied on members of the parish, usually based on households; not always popular and could lead to disputes (see Landscot).

Churchwardens

members of the congregation, usually elected on an annual basis around Easter and usually comprising two in number, who were responsible for the maintenance of the church during their term of office; they were also responsible for responding to visitation articles presented by their bishop or archdeacon, and such articles posed questions about all aspects of the life of the community from attendance at church to sexual misdemeanours.

Clapper   internal hammer that strikes a bell to create a sound.

Cloths, carpets and cushions   required to adorn the communion table, pulpit and some seats, which could be made from a variety of materials according to the wealth of the parish.

Communion Table   required in every church (Canon 82), moveable in the sixteenth century, more likely to be found in a fixed position in the chancel in the seventeenth century and railed, suggesting to many a return to 'altars'.

Consistory Court   the chief diocesan court conducted under the authority of a bishop; cases were split between 'office' cases brought by church officials and 'instance' cases brought by members of the public in actions against one another, the forerunner of modern civil law proceedings.

Curate   clergyman with the spiritual responsibility for the 'cure of souls' in a parish; the term could be applied to the incumbent or an assistant he appointed.

Decalogue   the ten commandments – a copy was required to be placed in the church (Canon 82).

Detection books   record of cases brought before the church courts.

Easter   one of the three prime church festivals and a day of obligation when all members of the congregation were expected to attend church and take communion; churchwardens were required to make presentments of those failing to attend and to comment particularly on Catholic recusants, those who steadfastly refused to attend and take communion.

Farmer   a person to whom the 'great tithes' were 'farmed out', often in the case where the impropriation was held by a corporation; it was the farmer who then became responsible for the costs of maintaining the chancel, but such people presumably felt that receipt of the great tithes was worth that risk, for as the returns for 1602 suggest, chancel repairs might be neglected.

Feast of the Annunciation	also known as 'Lady Day', 25 March.
Feast of St John the Baptist	birth 24 June; beheading 29 August.
Feast of St Michael the Archangel	29 September.
Feast of the Purification	also known as Candlemas, 2 February.
Flagon	large jug for water or wine.
Font	structure, usually stone, containing water used for baptism of children, often located towards the west end of the church and near a door, something favoured by Archbishop Laud who enquired if the font occupied its 'ancient place'; elaborate covers became fashionable in the seventeenth century – required by Canon 81.
Font Cover	see above and note occurrence of enquiries in 1636, but also earlier.
Glebe	property belonging to the living for the use of the incumbent: might often provide a 'glebe cottage', land used for the purpose of a 'cottage garden' and might comprise in total several acres, some of which might be used by local farmers and so provide a rental income (glebe averaged around 5 acres per parish in 1724).
Glebe Terrier	a document giving details of the 'glebe', drawn up by the churchwardens, noted in Canon 87, the survival of which for parishes seems to coincide particularly strongly with dates at which Metropolitical Visitations occurred.
Grip	a small furrow or ditch, a narrow cavity.
Grownepinninge	probably equivalent to underpinning, referring to foundations.

Hatchment	a diamond/lozenge shaped shield on which heraldic symbols were painted denoting key families of the parish buried in the church after having been carried at funeral services.
Healing	the action of covering something, hence chiefly associated with roof repairs; it might also mean the material used for the roof, such as slate or tile.
Hood	required for use by all ministers with a university degree
Horsham slab	a common roofing 'tile' found in Sussex, a rather large, rough hewn slab of stone.
Impropriation (see also appropriation)	the income derived from the 'great tithes' based on agricultural produce and livestock which went to the impropriator of a living or 'rector' who, if a laymen, had to supply the living with a suitable ordained minister who might be termed the vicar, parson or curate.
Incumbent	holder of an eccesiastical benefice/living.
King's Arms	see also Royal Coat of Arms below.
Lady Day	the Feast of the Annunciation, 25 March.
Landscot	a rate levied on households and landowners in the parish when major repairs of the church were necessary.
Lattice-(window)	a window made of small diamond-shaped panes set in lead-work.
Linsey-woolsey	a textile material, woven from a mixture of wool and flax; a dress material of coarse inferior wool, woven upon a cotton warp. [OED]
Litten	a churchyard.
Living	a clerical post to which an income was attached, often derived from endowments, glebe or tithes.
Michaelmas	the Feast of St Michael the Archangel, 29 September.

Metropolitical Visitation	a visitation carried out under the authority of either the Archbishop of Canterbury or of York governing their entire province.
Mullion	vertical stone or wooden division of a window.
Notary Public	a legal secretary/ professional scribe; one who serviced the church courts and other events by recording proceedings.
Outleat or outlett	a local term that seems to have been used to denote entrances and exits from the church, perhaps even the porches.
Ovis	dialect term for the 'eves' of a church, which often seemed to need closing to prevent rain water coming into the church.
Pace	a part of the floor raised by a step, a platform.
Pales	fencing found around churchyards, usually the responsibility of those with property abutting the yard to maintain.
Pargetting	decorative plaster work.
Partitions	or screens employed to separate the chancel from the nave; although some were removed on the Reformation, they were meant to be retained; often decorated with images of saints, which were covered up at the Reformation; above the screen was a rood loft (q.v.) and above that a rood (q.v.), a large crucifixion scene.
Paving/ pavement	the floor of a church, often found to be at fault in different parts of the church owing to use of aisles for burials and lack of boarding below pews; the surveys reveal that a number of churches still had earthen floors which would have been strewn with rushes.
Peculiar or exempt jurisdiction	a parish or number of parishes that were held in the jurisdiction of a person other than the 'ordinary' or bishop of the diocese in which they fell; these were therefore deemed to be 'exempt' from the jurisdiction of that ordinary, which might mean exemption from visitations (q.v.); in the archdeaconry of Chichester this applied to the Deanery of Pagham and Tarring (10 parishes) under the control of the Archbishops of Canterbury, and the Dean of Chichester's peculiar of nine

churches within the city and on its boundaries; approximately 11% of all of the 9,000 livings of England and Wales fell into such a category, but as many of these were controlled by other ecclesiastical authorities – as in Sussex – this need not have presented insuperable problems for the authorities.

Perambulations   walking/'beating' the parish boundaries traditionally held at Rogation Tide; occasions on which there was an obligation on outlying farms to provide cakes and ale for all who came.

Poor Man's Box   a small chest with a lock into which people could put alms for the poor of the parish (Canon 84).

Porch   porches became a common external feature of churches after the fifteenth century and could be large enough to be the site for weddings, the holding of schools, and for a small parish library to be constructed above.

Pulpit   an elevated desk from which a minister could give sermons or read a homily, often with a sounding board above to aid hearing; common after the sixteenth century when chiefly made out of wood rather than stone, and required by the Elizabethan injunctions.

Presentment   a statement or charge given to an ecclesiastical court by the churchwardens or minister regarding church matters ranging from the fabric to personal misbehaviour; usually made in answer to articles of enquiry raised for a visitation, but could be made at any time during the year and submitted to the bishop's consistory court; might often only be made on the basis of 'common fame'.

Quarrel   a square or diamond-shaped pane of glass, used in making lattice-windows (qv).

Quire   another term for the Choir or Chancel of a church.

Reading desk   a lectern usually with an attached seat from which the minister read the services of morning and evening prayer, and might also read much of the communion service; it might also be used as a place where schoolchildren might be taught.

Rector   clergyman or layman who received the great tithes of a living.

Registers the keeping of parish registers for baptisms, burials and weddings was required by law after 1538; other registers might include 'a register of strange preachers' in which the names of outside preachers should be noted to check if licensed; registers might be provided for inspection at times of visitation, along with licences.

Royal Coat of Arms coat of arms of holder of the crown, required in every church in the reign of Edward VI, but then not really enforced until that of Charles II, although good examples for Queen Elizabeth, James I and Charles I do survive in Sussex churches.

Rood a sculture or other depiction of Christ on the Cross often found on rood screens, above lofts within the chancel arch; removed in many churches in the reign of Edward VI, restored under Mary, but removed again under Elizabeth.

Rood loft a loft or gallery on top of the chancel screen, used in pre-Reformation times for devotional images and candles; although also served practical uses such as storage of parish weapons and equipment; such lofts were required to be taken down in the reign of Queen Elizabeth, an order resisted in many outlying parts of the country, for these frequently contained highly decorated and expensive woodwork.

Rushbearing the custom of cleaning and renewing floor rushes for the church usually practised on the day of the patron saint.

Screen see partition.

Sentences of Scripture required by Canon 82 after 1604 and included The Creed, the Ten Commandments and the Lord's Prayer, but could also include other texts, a favourite in the 1630s being the exhortation: 'Let all things be done decently and in good order'.

Shingles roofing material rather similar to tiles, but made out of wood.

Sidesmen assistants to the churchwardens at services and other parish activities; such people might eventually become churchwardens.

Skilling a shed or an outhouse.

Surplice

long, loose white vestment worn by the clergy over a cassock; controversial with many as 'the rags of Rome' but required by canon law.

Table of Degrees of Marriage and Affinity

list of the prohibited degrees of marriage required to be placed in open view, presumably near the church door or in the porch; required advice for all those seeking to be married; there appears to have been a campaign to ensure that they could be found in all churches in the 1630s.

Tithes

payments based on a 'tenth' of one's income derived from agricultural produce, manufacturing or sales, usually split between the 'great or rectoral tithes' arising from major items such as corn crops and 'small or vicarial tithes' arising from lesser items including the pasturage and produce of livestock. The system was complicated and clearly difficult to calculate, particularly in urban settings, and was eventually commuted into a more obvious form of financial taxation in the nineteenth century.

Terrier

see glebe terriers.

Utensils of the church

these would include communion cups, patens, flagons, etc., usually of silver by the seventeenth century, but also still of pewter.

Vestments

items of cloth, fine linen, etc., required for use of the minister when conducting service, notably a large surplice.

Visitation

inspection carried out under the authority of an archbishop, a bishop, diocesan chancellor, archdeacon or a rural dean, usually preceded by the issue of 'articles of enquiry' based on the Canons, but which might carry the special interests of particular bishops and others.

Whiting

term used to denote the need for limewashing the walls of a church, often used when also calling for 'beautification' (qv).

KEY PEOPLE INVOLVED IN THESE SURVEYS
FROM SENIOR FIGURES TO LOCAL OFFICIALS COVERING THE PERIOD 1600-1640

Archbishops of Canterbury

John Whitgift DD (c.1530-1604), Archbishop (1583-1604)   *ODNB*

Richard Bancroft DD (1544-1610), Archbishop (1604-10)   *ODNB*

George Abbot DD (1562-1633), Archbishop (1611-33)   *ODNB*

William Laud DD (1573-1645), Archbishop (1633- executed 1645)   *ODNB*

Bishops of Chichester

Anthony Watson DD (c.1549-1605), Bishop (1596-1605)   *ODNB*

Lancelot Andrewes DD (1555-1626), Bishop (1605-09)   *ODNB*

Samuel Harsnett DD (1561-1631), Bishop (1609-19)   *ODNB*

George Carleton DD (1559-1628), Bishop (1619-28)   *ODNB*

Richard Montagu DD (1577-1641) Bishop (1628-38)   *ODNB*

Brian Duppa DD (1589-1662) Bishop (1638-41)   *ODNB*

Diocesan Chancellors/ Vicars General

Anthony Blencowe DCL (d.1618), Diocesan Chancellor (1586-1607); Provost of Oriel College, Oxford (1572-1618); Oxford Diocesan Chancellor (1607-18)*ODNB*

Sir Nathaniel Brent DCL (1574-1652), Warden of Merton College, Oxford (1621-45); Vicar-General to Archbishop of Canterbury (1629-41); knighted 1639; conducted Laud's Metropolitical Visitation but fell out with the Archbishop over policy and later worked for Parliament.   *ODNB*

Clement Corbett (d.1652), Master of Trinity Hall, Cambridge (1611-26); Diocesan Chancellor (1614-27); Diocesan Chancellor of Norwich (1625-52)   *ODNB*

John Drury DCL (d.1614), Diocesan Chancellor (1607-14); Preb. Bishophurst (1582-1614); R Pulborough (1589-14); Archdeacon of Oxford (1592)   *ODNB*

William Neville DCL (1596-1640), Diocesan Chancellor and Dean's
Commissary (1627-40); Commissary for Lewes archdeaconry (1627-40);
JP 1635   *ODNB*

Sir Edward Stanhope LLD (c.1546-1608), Vicar-General to Archbishop of
Canterbury (1583-1608); Master in Chancery (1591-1608); Chancellor of London
diocese (1578-1608)   *ODNB*

Deans of Chichester Cathedral

Martin Culpepper DM (d.1605), Dean (1577-1601); Warden of New College,
Oxford (1573-1599)

William Thorne BD (c.1568-1630), Dean (1601-30); Regius Professor of Hebrew
at Oxford (1598-1604); active in Chichester courts   *ODNB*

Francis Dee DD (d.1638), Dean (1630-34), Bishop of Peterborough (1634-38)
                                                                 ODNB

Richard Steward DCL (c.1593-1651), Dean (1634-42); Clerk of the Closet (1638-
c.1646); Dean of St Paul's (1642-51)   *ODNB*

Chancellors of Chichester Cathedral

Henry Blaxton MA (c.1545-1606), Chancellor (1573-1606); Preb. Highleigh
(1570-71); Preb. West Wittering 1572-1606); Canon Res. (1572-1606); V Cocking
(1574-1606); R West Thorney (1573-1606); active in archdeaconry courts

Roger Andrewes BD (1574-1635), Chancellor (1606-35); Canon Res. (1609-35);
younger brother of Bishop Lancelot A.; Master of Jesus College, Cambridge
(1618-32); one of the translators of the new Bible; V Cocking (1606-09); R
Nuthurst (1606-09)

John Scull MA (d.1641), Chancellor (1635-41); Preb. Bracklesham (1629-32);
Preb. Waltham (1632-41); related to Bishop Montagu

Archdeacons of Chichester

Henry Ball DD (c.1553-1603), Archdeacon (1596-1603); Canon Res. (1593-1603);
Precentor (1582-96); Preb. Bursal (1593-1603); R Tangmere (1602-3)

Thomas Pattenson BD (d.1607), Archdeacon (1603-07)

Roger Andrewes BD (1574 -1635), Archdeacon (1608-35) [see above]

Lawrence Pay MA (d.1640), Archdeacon (1635-40), Canon Res. (1635-40)

Archdeacons of Lewes

John Mattock MA (d.1612), Archdeacon (1598-1612)

Richard Buckenham BD (d.1628), Archdeacon (1612-28), Canon Res. (1614-28); Preb. Eartham (1610-14); R Harting (1611-28); Preb. Bishophurst (1614-28)

William Hutchinson MA (d.1644), Archdeacon of Lewes (1628-44)

Civil lawyers and clergy acting as surrogates in the courts

Hugh Barker DCL (1565-1632), Commissary of Dean's Peculiar (1602-11); Highleigh Prebendary (1590-c.1604); member of national Court of Delegates between 1608 and 1632; Official of the archdeacon of Oxford in 1618 and succeeded Blencowe as Chancellor of that diocese. *ODNB*

Francis Coxe DD (d.1613), Canon Res. (1570-1613); Preb. Hova Parva (1587-1613); Warden St Mary's Hospital, Chichester (1602-13), R Slindon (1598-1613); active in running courts in 1602-3 & again in 1610; Preb. Seaford (1573-85); R New Fishbourne (1597-1613); R Headley (1586-97)

William Coxe BA (d.1632), Canon Res. (1616-32); Preb. Somerley (1611-32); R Headley (1597-1632); active in Pagham & Tarring courts

George Edgley MA (d.1644), Preb. Heathfield (1633-44); V Donnington (1630-44); V Lyminster (1634-44); active in archdeaconry courts in the 1630s

Thomas Emerson (d.1635), Canon Res. (1626-34); Preb. Hamstead (1609-35); V of Hunston & V of Climping; active in Pagham & Tarring courts

Robert Johnson BD (d.1640), Preb. Firle 1624-40, R St Andrew, Chichester (1625-37), R St Olave, Chichester (1625-37), royal chaplain to King James I; active in running archdeaconry courts in the 1630s

Richard Kitson BA (d.1602), Canon Res. (1571-1602); Preb. Bracklesham (1564-1602); Warden St Mary's Hospital, Chichester (1580-1602); R Tangmere (1588-1602); active in Pagham & Tarring courts & archdeaconry

William Lawes (d.1622), R St Peter the Less, Chichester, (1596-1605); signed off the 1603 survey of Chichester churches; R East Wittering (1613-22)

Thomas Leame (d.1606), R St Andrew, Chichester, active in running courts in 1602-3, R St Pancras (1568-70), R St Peter the Great (1591-1606)

Martin Okin BD, R East Lavant (1610-12); active in Pagham & Tarring courts

Joshua Pieto MA, (d.1662) R of All Saints, Chichester (c.1619-40s); active in running Pagham & Tarring courts in 1630s

Francis Ringsted LLB (d.1649), Dean of Peculiar of Pagham & Tarring (1625-42)

Thomas Scales MA (active 1600s) Commissary and Official for Dean & Chp.

Owen Stockton MA (d. 1626), R. East Lavant (1612-26); active in running courts for Pagham & Tarring

Garrett Williamson BD (d.1610), Canon Res. (1602-10); Preb Mardon (1596-1610), R East Lavant (1601-10); active in running Pagham & Tarring courts

Notaries and registrars

Richard Juxon (d.1612), Notary Public; Diocesan and Chapter Registrar 1597-1612

Thomas Juxon (active 1600s), Notary Public; Chapter Registrar (1615)

Edward Osborne (active in 1630s) Notary Public

Richard Stanley (active in 1630s), Notary Public

George Stent (active in 1600s), Notary Public

John Swayne (c.1590-1654) Notary Public; Deputy Chapter Clerk (1613)

Christopher Thecker (active 1600s) Notary Public

TABLE OF CHURCHES AND CHAPELS COVERED BY THE SURVEYS IN ALPHABETICAL ORDER
FOLLOWED BY CHURCHES OF THE DEAN OF CHICHESTER'S PECULIAR AND CHURCHES OF THE PECULIAR OF PAGHAM AND TARRING

CHURCH		DEANERY	1602	1610	1636	GLEBE TERRIER	KB-VALUE
Aldingbourne		Boxgrove	✓	✓	✓	1615/1635	£10
Amberley		Arundel	✓	✓	✓	1615	£7
Angmering	R	Arundel	✓	✓	✓	1615/1635	£16
Appledram		Boxgrove	✓	✓	✓	1615/1635	£15
Arundel		Arundel	✓	✓	✓	1615/1635	£39
Ashington	R	Storrington	✓	✓	✓	1615/1635	£8
Ashurst	R	Storrington	✓	✓	✓	1615/1635	-
Barlavington	R	Midhurst	✓	✓	✓	1615/1635	£29
Barnham		Arundel	✓	✓	✓	1615/1635	£7
Bepton	R	Midhurst	✓	✓	✓	1615/1635	£8
Bignor	R	Midhurst	✓	✓	✓	1615/1635	£8
Billingshurst		Storrington	✓	✓	✓	1635	£9
Binderton		Boxgrove	✓	✓	✓		-
Binsted	R	Arundel	✓	o	✓	1615/1635	£40
Birdham	R	Boxgrove	✓	✓	✓	1615/1635	£10
Bosham		Boxgrove	✓	✓	✓	1635	£48
Botolphs		Storrington	✓	✓	✓	1615/1635	-
Boxgrove		Boxgrove	✓	✓	✓	1615/1635	£9
Bramber	R	Storrington	✓	✓	✓	1615/1635	£45
Broadwater	R	Storrington	✓	✓	o		£36
Buncton		Storrington	✓	o	✓	1615/1635	-
Burpham		Arundel	✓	o	✓	1615	£39
Burton	R	Midhurst	o	o	✓	1635	£38
Bury		Arundel	✓	✓	✓	1635	£13
Chidham		Boxgrove	✓	✓	✓	1635	£27
Chilgrove		Boxgrove	✓	o	o		-
Chithurst		Midhurst	✓	✓	✓	1635	-
Clapham	R	Arundel	✓	✓	✓	1615	£30
Climping		Arundel	✓	✓	✓	1615/1635	£10
Coates		Midhurst	✓	o	✓	1615	-
Cocking		Midhurst	✓	o	✓	1615/1635	£13

CHURCH		DEANERY	1602	1610	1636	GLEBE TERRIER	KB-VALUE
Coldwaltham		Midhurst	✓	✓	✓	1615/1635	£7
Compton	R	Boxgrove	✓	✓	✓		£13
Coombes	R	Storrington	✓	✓	✓	1615/1635	£10
Didling		Midhurst	✓	o	✓	1615/1635	-
Donnington		Boxgrove	✓	✓	✓	1615/1635	£10
Duncton	R	Midhurst	✓	o	✓	1615	-
Earnley	R	Boxgrove	✓	✓	✓	1615/1635	£7
Eartham		Boxgrove	✓	✓	✓	1615/1635	-
Easebourne		Midhurst	✓	✓	✓	1635	£6
East Dean	R	Boxgrove	✓	✓	✓	1615	£29
East Marden	R	Boxgrove	✓	✓	o		£38
East Preston		Arundel	✓	✓	✓		-
East Wittering	R	Boxgrove	✓	✓	✓	1635	£42
Eastergate	R	Arundel	✓	✓	✓	1615/1635	£8
Egdean	R	Midhurst	o	o	✓		£21
Elsted	R	Midhurst	✓	✓	✓	1615/1635	£11
Felpham	R	Arundel	✓	✓	✓	1615	£20
Fernhurst		Midhurst	✓	✓	o		-
Ferring		Arundel	✓	✓	✓	1635	£46
Findon		Storrington	✓	✓	✓	1615/1635	£20
Fittleworth	R	Midhurst	✓	✓	✓	1635	£7
Ford	R	Arundel	✓	✓	✓	1615/1635	£27
Funtington		Boxgrove	✓	✓	✓	1615	£23
Goring		Storrington	✓	✓	✓	1615/1635	£47
Graffham	R	Midhurst	✓	✓	✓	1635	£10
Greatham	R	Storrington	✓	✓	✓		-
Hardham	R	Midhurst	✓	✓	✓	1635	£6
Heyshott		Midhurst	✓	✓	✓	1615/1635	-
Horsham		Storrington	✓	✓	✓	1615/1635	£25
Houghton		Arundel	✓	✓	✓	1635	-
Hunston		Boxgrove	✓	✓	✓	1615/1635	£9
Iping	R	Midhurst	✓	✓	✓	1615/1635	£7
Itchingfield	R	Storrington	✓	✓	✓	1615/1635	£8
Kingston	R	Arundel	✓	✓	o		-
Kirdford		Midhurst	✓	o	✓	1615/1635	£11
Lancing		Storrington	✓	✓	✓	1615/1635	£26

CHURCH		DEANERY	1602	1610	1636	GLEBE TERRIER	KB-VALUE
Linchmere		Midhurst	✓	✓	o	1615/1635	£3
Littlehampton		Arundel	✓	o	✓	1635	-
Lodsworth		Midhurst	✓	o	✓	1615/1635	-
Lordington		Boxgrove	✓	o	o		-
Lurgashall	R	Midhurst	✓	o	✓	1615/1635	£8
Lyminster		Arundel	✓	✓	✓	1615/1635	£9
Madehurst		Arundel	✓	✓	✓	1615/1635	£18
Merston	R	Boxgrove	✓	o	✓	1635	£7
Mid Lavant		Boxgrove	✓	✓	✓	1615	-
Middleton	R	Arundel	✓	✓	✓	1615	£41
Midhurst		Midhurst	✓	✓	✓		-
North Marden	R	Boxgrove	✓	✓	o		£36
North Mundham		Boxgrove	✓	✓	✓	1615/1635	£44
North Stoke		Arundel	✓	✓	✓	1615	£6
Northchapel	R	Midhurst	✓	o	✓	1615/1635	-
Nuthurst	R	Storrington	✓	o	✓	1615/1635	£10
Oving		Boxgrove	✓	✓	✓	1635	£11
Parham	R	Storrington	✓	✓	✓	1615/1635	£34
Petworth	R	Midhurst	✓	✓	✓	1615/1635	£42
Poling		Arundel	✓	✓	✓	1615/1635	£49
Pulborough	R	Storrington	o	o	o		£19
Racton	R	Boxgrove	✓	o	✓		£36
Rogate		Midhurst	o	✓	✓	1615	£48
Rudgwick		Storrington	✓	o	o		£13
Rusper	R	Storrington	✓	o	✓	1615/1635	£10
Rustington		Arundel	✓	✓	✓	1635	£29
Selham	R	Midhurst	✓	✓	✓	1615/1635	£40
Selsey	R	Boxgrove	✓	o	✓	1615	£11
Shipley		Storrington	✓	o	✓	1635	-
Sidlesham		Boxgrove	✓	✓	✓	1635	£27
Singleton	R	Boxgrove	✓	✓	✓	1615/1635	£50
Slinfold	R	Storrington	✓	✓	✓	1615/1635	£5
Sompting		Storrington	✓	✓	✓	1615/1635	£40
South Harting	R	Midhurst	✓	o	✓	1615/1635	£27

CHURCH		DEANERY	1602	1610	1636	GLEBE TERRIER	KB-VALUE
South Stoke	R	Arundel	✓	o	✓	1615	£12
Stedham	R	Midhurst	✓	o	✓	1615/1635	£18
Steyning		Storrington	✓	✓	✓	1635	£15
Stopham	R	Midhurst	o	✓	✓	1615/1635	£40
Storrington	R	Storrington	✓	✓	✓	1615/1635	£18
Stoughton		Boxgrove	✓	o	✓	1615/1635	£27
Sullington	R	Storrington	✓	o	✓	1615/1635	£13
Sutton	R	Midhurst	✓	✓	✓	1615/1635	£15
Terwick	R	Midhurst	✓	✓	✓	1615/1635	£46
Thakeham	R	Storrington	✓	o	o		£14
Tillington	R	Midhurst	✓	o	✓	1615/1635	£14
Tortington		Arundel	✓	o	✓	1635	-
Treyford	R	Midhurst	✓	o	✓	1615/1635	£7
Trotton	R	Midhurst	✓	o	✓	1615	£9
Tuxlith		Midhurst	✓	o	o		-
Upmarden		Boxgrove	✓	✓	✓	1615/1635	-
Upwaltham	R	Boxgrove	✓	o	✓	1615	£41
Walberton		Arundel	✓	✓	✓	1615/1635	£49
Warminghurst		Storrington	✓	✓	✓	1615/1635	-
Warnham		Storrington	✓	✓	✓	1615/1635	£10
Warningcamp		Arundel	✓	✓	✓		-
Washington		Storrington	✓	✓	✓	1615	£30
West Chiltington	R	Storrington	✓	✓	✓	1615/1635	£13
West Dean		Boxgrove	✓	✓	✓	1615	£28
West Grinstead	R	Storrington	✓	✓	✓	1615/1635	£26
West Itchenor	R	Boxgrove	✓	✓	✓	1615/1635	£32
West Stoke	R	Boxgrove	✓	✓	✓	1615/1635	£49
West Thorney	R	Boxgrove	✓	o	o		£10
West Wittering		Boxgrove	✓	✓	✓	1615	£30
Westbourne	R	Boxgrove	✓	o	✓	1615/1635	£39
Westhampnett		Boxgrove	✓	✓	✓	1615/1635	£20
Wiggonholt	R	Storrington	✓	✓	✓	1615/1635	£7

CHURCH		DEANERY	1602	1610	1636	GLEBE TERRIER	KB-VALUE
Wisborough Green		Storrington	✓	o	✓	1615/1635	£45
Wiston	R	Storrington	✓	✓	✓	16/1635	£13
Woolavington	R	Midhurst	✓	✓	✓	1615/1635	£9
Woolbeding	R	Midhurst	✓	o	✓	1615/1635	£7
Yapton		Arundel	✓	✓	✓	1615/1635	£44

The Dean of Chichester's Peculiar

CHURCH			1602	1610	1636	GLEBE TERRIER	KB-VALUE
Fishbourne	R		✓	o	o		£6
Rumboldswhyke	R		✓	o	o		£38
St Andrew	R		✓	o	o		£8
St Bartholomew	R		✓	✓	o		£2
St Martin	R		✓	o	o		£5
St Olave	R		✓	✓	o		£20
St Pancras	R		✓	✓	o		£15
St Peter the Great (Subdeanery)			✓	✓	o		£30
St Peter the Less	R		✓	✓	o		£18

Peculiar of Pagham and Tarring

CHURCH			1602	1610	1636	GLEBE TERRIER	KB-VALUE
All Saints Chichester	R		✓	o	o	1627/1635	£11
Bersted			✓	o	o	1617/1625	£8
Durrington			✓	o	o	1636	-
East Lavant	R		✓	o	o	1615/1635	£21
Heene			✓	o	o	1636	-
Pagham			✓	o	o	1626/1635	£10
Patching	R		✓	o	o	1615/1635	£12
Slindon	R		✓	o	o	1632/1635	£15
Tangmere	R		✓	o	o	1615/1635	£13
Tarring	R		✓	o	o	1615/1636	£23

Note: R indicates that the living was a rectory

MAP

DEPICTING THE PARISHES OF THE ARCHDEACONRY OF CHICHESTER, ALSO DENOTING RURAL DEANERY BOUNDARIES AND PECULIAR JURISDICTIONS

MAP OF THE ARCHDEACONRY OF CHICHESTER SHOWING
THE RURAL DEANERIES AND THE PECULIARS OF
PAGHAM & TARRING (ARCHBISHOP OF CANTERBURY)
AND CHICHESTER (DEAN)

TEXT FROM SURVIVING SURVEYS
FOR CHURCHES AND CHAPELS IN THE ARCHDEACONRY OF CHICHESTER

IN ALPHABETICAL ORDER

FOLLOWED BY

CHURCHES OF THE DEAN OF CHICHESTER'S PECULIAR
CHURCHES OF THE PECULIAR OF PAGHAM AND TARRING

TOGETHER WITH PHOTOGRAPHS FROM THE PETRIE, WALKER AND BARHAM COLLECTIONS

Aldingbourne – St Mary   *Boxgrove Deanery*

Incumbent	Patron (where known)
1602 – Alan Thomson	William Kitching by grant Dean & Chapter
1610 – Alan Thomson	
1636 – Daniel Thompson	Richard Gunter

1602   (impropriator/farmer: John Elson)

The Chauncell is ruinous in the roofe & healing
the glasewindows are brocken and some unglased
the walles are indecaye and unseemely
the pavementes faltie and some of yt unpaved

The Churche is faltie in the healing and gutters,
the glasse windowes are faltie
the pavementes are faltie
the walles are undecent
there is no pulpett but the place where prayers is reade
the fonte will hold no water
the seates are indefalte & some broken
the grounde unseemely
the window in the Church porche is unglased
the south doore & the key of the doore is broken
the partition between the Church & Chancel is very unseemely

30 October 1610

The Church in decay in the roofe and the windowes in the north side

25 November 1636

All the Northside of the Churchyard wantes to be new fenced.
The Church wantes to be all new whited & beautified with Sentences of
Scripture, & the Kings Armes to be fairly sett up in the Church.

There wantes a new Surplace ~~and hood~~
for the Minister & a better lynnen
Cloth for the Communion Table, &
alsoe a better Carpett for the
Communion Table.

There wantes a Cloth and Cushion for
the Pulpett.

There is noe note indented of the
utensilles of the Church, nor a book of
Canons, nor a Booke for the 5th of
November.

There are 4 or 5 great Cracks in the Church walls which if they be not speedily
amended willbee the ruyn of the Church.

The Church doth greatly want reparing in the Covering.

All the Seates in the Chauncell want to be boarded or paved in the Bottoms.

There are dunghills & heapes of rubbidge lying in the Churchyard.

There is Noe Table of the degrees of marriage.

There wantes two faire Flaggons for the Communion wyne.

There wantes a Cover for the Font, and a new dore to the Church porch.

There are divers Seates at the lower end of the Church which are very ruynous
and the most part of the Seates in the Church want to be plancked or Boarded.

Amberley – St Michael

Arundel Deanery

Incumbent	Patron (where known)
1602 – John Scarborough	Bishop of Chichester
1610 – James Hutchenson	
1636 – Henry Manners	

1602

The Chancel roofe is in defalte there be divers drippes
the timber work is decayed
the whole roofe is sunck from the Church wall at the east ende with the [bueh?]
thereof that it seemeth to be dangerous in the whole [building?]
the flowere beinge of earthe is broken

The Church hath in it divers drippes
the walls want whitinge
sertayne places under the roofe are to be stopped to kepe out pigions
ii glasse windows broken one the glasse beinge gon hathe in it a lettice another
two leaves of wood
the timber & masons marke above the fonte in decaye certaine of the seates in
the timber worke & under foote undecent
the flowere is broken one other side of the Church
the paving in defalte
the walls [in] defalte
the tower in decay in walinge in the covering in leadinge in the timber worke
it wanteth a dore the toppe & bordes in the upper lofte
the porch is faltie in the roofe and grownepinninge

30 October 1610

To certify faults & repair

11 November 1636

The Church wantes to be adorned
with Sentences of Scripture.
The Seates on both sides of the
Chauncell want to be paved or
boarded in the bottomes.
Some of the seates in the Chauncell
stand equall with the Communion Table on both sides.
The Communion Booke is not of the last edition.
There is not the Booke for the 5th of November.
~~The Chauncell wantes beautifying with Sentences of Scripture.~~
~~There is noe hood for the Minister~~, nor Table of the degrees of marriage.
There is noe note indented of the utensills of the Church.
There wantes twoe Flaggons for the Communion wyne, there being 200
Communicants in the parish.
The Church porch wantes paveing.
There is noe Chest for Alms for the poore.

Angmering – St Margaret   *Arundel Deanery*

Incumbent	Patron (where known)
1602 – Michael Jones	Sir Thomas Palmer
1610 – Michael Jones	
1636 – Edward Blaxton	Sir Edward Bishop

1602

The seates want paving or plancking in the bottom
there is a littell Chancel one the northe side of the olyes that hath neede to be repaired in the covering selinge glass windowes and paving

The seates have neede all of them to be new made and sett closer together
the bottomes want plancking
the paving also in both the iles is decayed
the windowes & a window at the east ende of the south ile the covering of the Church especially at the south ile have need to be repaired
the walles to be whited there wanteth a pulpitt dore & a covering for the fonte
the sealing also from the Chauncel dore downe into the Church have neede of mendinge

30 October 1610

The south west corner of the Church in decaye, and the Munnyons of the Church windowes faultie the communion table undecent

11 November 1636

The Churchyard wantes fencing round about.
The walls of the Chauncell want plaistring & whiteing.
There is a place on the left hand of the Chauncell which wantes paveing.
They want a new Communion Booke & a booke of homilies and a cloth and Cushion for the Pulpett, the old being very badd
There is not the Service Booke for the 5th of November nor Table of the degrees of marriage, nor note indented of the Utensills of the Church.
The Seate on the left side of the Chauncell wantes to be paved & Boarded in the bottome.
There wantes a dore to the Pulpett.

Appledram – St Mary the Virgin   *Boxgrove Deanery*

Incumbent	Patron (where known)
1602 – William Payne	Dean & Chapter
1610 – Constantine Turton	
1636 – Constantine Turton	

1602   *(impropriator/farmer: John Ryman)*

The north flower is not paved
the windows lacke scowring and the walles whitinge

The yles not paved
the seates be in muche decaye and want plancking
the pulpit standeth weakely and wanteth a doore
the flower is much broken

22 October 1610

The Church porch verie much decayed the Churchyard unrepaired

[November] 1636

The Churchyard must be better fenced
A New Communion table with a cloth & Carpett
A New Book of Homilies
A better Reading place for the minister
A new pulpit cloth & Cushion
To make an indented note of the Utinsells of the Church

Arundel – St Nicholas *Arundel Deanery*

Incumbent	Patron (where known)
1602 – William Carver	Crown
1610 – William Carver	
1636 – Thomas Heyney	John Wilson

1602

The Chancell windows are very much broken

There are fower seates in the lower ende of the Churche
the wall of the tower is sumwhat decayed a little falte or two in the pavement
the west porche wanteth croftes

30 October 1610

The Church wanteth coveringe the munyions of the windowes faultie & the leades somewhat drippie

11 November 1636

There wantes a new Carpett & Cloth for the Communion Table and a new Cloth & Cushion for the Pulpett.
The Church wantes to be beautified with sentences of Scripture.
There wantes another Flaggon for the Communion wyne & a Service Booke for the 5th of November.
There wantes a new Surplace; the old being very badd.

Ashington – St Peter and St Paul   *Storrington Deanery*

Incumbent	Patron (where known)
1602 – Christopher Minshull	Crown
1610 – Christopher Minshull	
1636 – Thomas Carr	

1602

The Chancel wanteth pavinge and washing

The Church wanteth pavinge and the walls whiting
the windows lacke some glasinge the seates are bottomlesse

3 November 1610

The communion table undecent the glass windowes faultie, & there wants a
bible the bell frame rotten & faultie no preaching pulpett nor reading pulpett

6 December 1636

The Communion Table is not railed in. There are Seates standing in the
Chauncell in equall height with the Communion Table.
The Carpett for the Communion Table is very old & full of great holes.
The healing of the Chauncell wantes reparing & the Chauncell windowes are
broken.
There wantes a new Booke of Common Praier.
The Seates in the Church want reparing & the Church windowes are much
broken.
The healing of the Church wantes mending.
They have not the Booke of homilies nor the booke of Canons nor Table of the
degrees of marriage.
The Fence of the Churchyard is much at decay so that hogges come in at many
places.
The Churchyard is much overgrowne with Bushes.
They have noe Chest for Almes for the poore, ~~nor hood for the Minister, he
being a Batchellor of Artes.~~
~~The Floore of the Church porch is unpaved & lyeth very undecent.~~
They want a faire flaggon for the Communion wyne.

Ashurst – St James
Storrington Deanery

Incumbent	Patron (where known)
1602 – Beda Goodacres	Sir Thomas Shirley
1610 – Beda Goodacres	
1636 – William Stonnard	

1602   *(impropriator/farmer: Beda Goodacres)*

The Chancel is well save that the flower is unpaved

The upper wall over the Chancel is not decayed but wolde be better pargeted and trimed

the seates most of them very ruinous and badd

the flower unpaved

the font is very badd and ruinos and standeth in a very inconvenient place out of the face of the Church and the sight of the greatest of the congregacion

3 November 1610

The north side of the Church wanteth pointinge the south west buttress in decay & the est side & ridges of the Church faultie & north west end also

25 November 1636

The Communion Table is not railed in.

The Pavement of the Chancel is to be raised higher where the Communion Table is to stand.

There are some Seats which stand to neere to the Communion Table to be removed and set farther of.

The Fence of the Churchyard is insufficient in many places.

There is some defect in the healing of the Chauncell.

There the Register Booke is not kept in the Church in the Chest but at the Parsons howse.

They want a Comely Flaggon for the Communion wyne.

They want the Booke of homilies and a Table of the degrees of marriage.

They have noe chest for Alms for the poore.

Barlavington – St Mary   *Midhurst Deanery*

Incumbent	Patron (where known)
1602 – Henry Duppa	Crown
1610 – Henry Duppa	Crown
1636 – John Randall	Katherine Beeding by grant of William Goring of Burton

1602   *(impropriator/farmer: Henry Duppa)*

The Church lacketh paving whitinge and glasinge
the south side of the Church to be po[inted?]
the seats to be plancked and some seats to be mended
there lacketh a better communion table a more comly pupitt
there lacketh a brasse [?] for their bells

30 October 1610

The steple like to fall, the Church and porch in decay in covering

25 November 1636

The Churchyard wantes fencing at the East end.
The Church windows of the Church and Chauncell are broken in divers places.
~~The Ten Commaundments are not fairly sett up on the walls of the Church nor any Sentences of Scripture.~~
The Communion Table is altogether unfit for that place.
The Chauncell wantes much reparing in the covering thereof.
There wantes a more comely seat for the Minister and the Pulpett is very unfitting.
The Seates in the Church and Chauncell are altogether ruined
~~The Floore of the Church wantes paving almost in every place.~~
~~The Pavement in the South Isle of the Church is suncke & must be paved or raised.~~
There is no Bill indented of the utensills of the Church.

Barnham – St Mary   *Arundel Deanery*

Incumbent	Patron (where known)
1602 – Garrett Scoree	Sir John Shelley
1610 – Thomas Meoles	
1636 – Thomas Meoles	

1602   *(impropriator/farmer: John Cooper)*

The Chancel glasse windows are in default
some wante of pavinge

The seates of the Church are to be mended
some places nedeth pavinge
the particion to be made up [ ] through and whited

30 October 1610

The Church in decay in tymber & wanteth subporters to strengthen them

25 November 1636

All the North side of the Churchyard wantes to be new fenced.
The Chauncell wantes to be beawtified.
The Church wantes to be new whited & the Ten commaundements & the
Kinges Armes to be fairly sett up with other sentences of Scripture in the
Church.
Noe Cloth or Cushion for the Pulpett, nor Booke of Cannons nor Booke for the
5th of November, nor a note indented of the utensills of the Church nor a
Carpett for the Communion Table.
The Steeple wantes to be new boarded.
A new Cover for the Font.
There wantes a new dore to the North side of the Church the old being broken
and quite ruynated.

Bepton – St Mary   *Midhurst Deanery*

Incumbent	Patron (where known)
1602 – Thomas Goodwin	N. Fennick by grant of Viscount Montague
1610 – William Ruffe	Thomas Hitchcock
1636 – William Ruffe	

1602   *(impropriator/farmer: Thomas Goodwin)*

The roofe of the Chancell one the south side is at defalte and requireth wasshinge
there are two rentes in the wall of one of the northe windowes
the parsons seate ruinous and unpaved
~~the Communion Table unseemly~~
the wall without is at default

The Church in parte unpaved & the seates unplancked
the walles want morteringe and whasshing
the steeple decayed the parsons seate where he reads pr[a]iers unconvenient
one window unglased
ij windows want repairing to be repaired by the Churchwardens
the communion table unseemly

30 October 1610

The Church in decay in healinge & the rooffe of the Church faulty in the timber

25 November 1636

The Chauncell wantes some whiteing & is not adorned with sentences of the Scripture.
The Church wantes whiteing throughout.
The Ten Commaundments and Sentences of Scripture which are sett up in the Church are quite worne out.
The Seates in the Chauncell want Boarding.
The Seates in the Church want paveing or plancking in the bottoms.
They have noe Table of the degrees of marriage, nor Service Booke for the 5th of November, nor note indented of the utensills of the Church.
There is noe Flaggon for the Communion wyne, nor cloth for the Pulpett.

Bignor – Holy Cross

Incumbent	Patron (where known)
1602 – William Burrell	Crown
1610 – William Burrell	
1636 – Edward Hastler	

1602

The Church lacketh pavinge glasing and whitinge

the seates to be made even underneath

the fonte lacketh mendinge

the bells to be better hanged and there is on the north side of the Church a particion which is called the chauntery which wolde be better sealed

30 October 1610

The steeple and porch in decay in the healing & timber

a window in the west end of the Church stopped up with stone

25 November 1636

The Communion Table is not railed in.

There wantes a new Communion Table & a bigger & more substantiall Flaggon for the Communion wyne.

~~They have not the booke of Canons.~~

~~The walls of the Church want whiteing in the inside & to be beautified with sentences of Scripture.~~

~~The Chauncell walls also want whiteing.~~

The Font will not hold water & is [very?] defective.

There are heapes of Rubbish in the Churchyard to be carried away.

The Church porch is in much decay.

The Church ~~porch~~ yard wantes fencing almost in every part hereof,

There wantes a new Carpett for the Communion Table.

They have not a beere to carry the dead to Church.

The ~~Seates in the Church want all reparacions. And when they are made they are to be soe sett that the people may kneele toward the East.~~

Billingshurst – St Mary   *Storrington Deanery*

Incumbent	Patron (where known)
1602 – Anthony Hilton	Henry Goring
1610 – Anthony Hilton	
1636 – Nathaniel Hilton	

1602

Some stones slipde from the covering
a few shingles sliped from the steeple
the chaple wanteth some pavement
the windowes want glasse
a rent throughe the wall that is in the ayle annexed unto the north parte of the
Church
the seates not plancked

3 November 1610

The south est ile faultie in healinge the
northest corner crackt the north
buttresses faultie the porch unpointed
& the Church alsoe

6 December 1636

The Communion Table standeth in Mr
Goring's Chauncell where there are
divers seates standing about. It were
fittest to remove it into parish

Chauncell, except Mr Goring will give way to have it set at the upper end of his Chauncell & to remove his Seates which stand about it.

~~There is noe raile about the Communion Table where it now standeth.~~

~~They want twoe Pewter Flaggons more for the Communion wyne besides that which they have already of Silver.~~

They have noe Chest for almes for the poore.

The pavement of the parish Chauncell wantes mending.

The Fence of the Churchyard is at default in many places soe that litle hogges Come in betweene the railes.

There ~~are~~ Ivy ~~Bushes~~, trees, bushes & other Shrubbs groweing in the walls of the Steeple which may in tyme be a meanes of the decay thereof.

Binderton – (no known dedication)   *Boxgrove Deanery*

Incumbent

1602 – Richard Hickes

1610 – Richard Hickes

1636 – Richard Hickes

1602   *(impropriator/farmer: William Smith)*

The Chauncell wanteth some pavinge
the windoes are unglased and some of the rough [roof] unhealed

The Church lacketh some paving and mendinge of the wall one the northside
the fonte wanteth a cover

20 October 1610

We present our steeple is in default for want of shinggle and our Church
windowes both want glasinge and the pavement of our Church is verie much
broken we likewise have no pulpitt and our communion cloth is verie bad and
unseemly for the place

22 October 1610

No chest to keepe the Register booke the north side of the Church and the
porch unrepaired, no pulpett the communion table verie badd

25 November 1636

The Church & Chauncell want to be whited throughout & be beautified with
Sentences of Scripture. Also the Ten Commaundments and the Kings Armes
are to be set up in the Church.
The 3 windowes in the Chauncell doe all want glaceing.
There wantes a new Communion Booke.
There is no Cloth nor Cushion for the Pulpett.
Noe particion betweene the Church & Chauncell.
Divers of the seats in the Church wantes reparing. And all the seats in the
Church want plancking or paveing.
There is noe Beere to carry the dead to buriall.
The Font will not hould water.
The Church wantes paveing in divers places.
They have noe Book of homilies, nor booke for the 5th of November nor note
indented of the Utensills of the Church.
The register Booke is not kept in the Church.
There is noe Flaggon for the Communion wyne.

Binsted – St Mary   *Arundel Deanery*

Incumbent	Patron (where known)
1602 – William Gandwell	Sir John Carell
1610 – William Gandwell	
1636 – Robert Johnson	William Neville by grant of Sir Garrett Kempe of Slindon

1602   *(impropriator/farmer: William Gandwell)*

The Chancel wanteth paving glasinge and payntinge

The Church windows are to be glased
the seates bothe to be repaired [?] and made decent
the Communion Table is not seemly
the Bible old and not of the translation required

25 November 1636

They have not the Booke for the 5th of November.
There wantes a new Surplace for the Minister.
They have noe note indented of the utensills of the Church.
There wantes a new Communion Booke; That which they have is not of the last edicion.

Birdham – St James   *Boxgrove Deanery*

Incumbent	Patron (where known)
1602 – John Waterhouse	Dean and Chapter
1610 – Humphrey Booth	
1636 – Adrian Dee	

1602   *(impropriator/farmer: John Waterhouse)*

The Chancel is very badly paved
the walles in some places beneth muldered downe
the windows are halfe damed upp

The Church wanteth pavinge and
the seates are many of them undecent & weake
the flower of them underfote very rough
the Churche walles are muche out of order
the plasteringe is muldered downe
the windows be divers of them muche damed up
the north dore is cleane dammed upp
ij seates with deskes at the particion betweene the Church and Chauncel are
like to fall downe
the fonte wanteth a good cover and the floreworke is muche refte and cloven
there is no 2nd pulpitt to preache in
the partition walle betwene the Churche and the belfrye is very rough in the
Churcheside nether plaistered nor whited

22 October 1610

The pulpett undecent, manie of the
windows of the Church in parte
stopped up the porch ill covered the
Church in decay in covering & a cracke
in the wall

[November] 1636

A better Carpett and linen clothe for the Communion table.

The Church porch wants paving.

A bigger and more decent Communion table.

A new surplice & better clothe for the pulpett.

The Church wants pavinge the Church wants plastring and whitinge

no table of degrees of marriage

no Booke of homilies and no indented note of the utensells of the Church;

to se that the beles be kept in good order to be new borded or paved

the belfre to bee new paved and the Church to bee paved where yt wantes and

to newe repaire the fonte and the half pace about yt

all the south side of the Churchyard wantes palinge or railing

the steeple to be new repaired;

the Church windowes wantes makeinge cleane and mending.

Bosham – Holy Trinity   *Boxgrove Deanery*

Incumbent	Patron (where known)
1602 – William Hide	Crown
1610 – Stephen Goldinge	John Shirley
1636 – George Horseman	Dean and Chapter, Chichester

1602   *(impropriator/farmer: William Hildrop)*

The Chancell [page torn] and the walles without to be [repaired] and mended
The Church pavement wanteth mending the seates are not decent
the windowes in many places unglased and the Churche porche neither
strongly walled nor well slatted

22 October 1610

The vestrie verie noisom and ill kept in the default of [the] Dean &
Churchwardens or his farmers

25 November 1636

There wantes a dore to the Pulpett.
~~The Minister saith that the reading place standeth not Conveniently for the Congregacion.~~
There wantes a new lynnen Clothe and Carpett for the Communion Table.
The Chauncell wantes paveing in many places.
The Seats on both sides of the Chauncell want paveing.
They have noe note indented of the Utensills of the Church, nor booke for the
5th of November, nor chest for Almes for the poore.
The belfrey wantes much reparing in the Covering. Also it wantes to be new paved.
The glasse windowes in the Chauncell want glaceing.
There is a grave in the Chauncell suncke and wantes to be raised.
The North Isle of the Church wantes paveing.
Many of the Seats in the Church wantes boarding & paving.
There wantes twoe new Flaggons for the Communion wyne, there being about
200 Communicants.
The Challice is not uniforme nor cleanly kept.
There is noe Table of the degrees of marriage.

Botolphs – St Botolph   *Storrington Deanery*

Incumbent	Patron (where known)
1602	Bishop of Chichester
1610 – James Wrench	
1636	

1602   *(impropriator/farmer: Bernard Parsons)*

The Chancel wanteth poyntinge in one place of the healing thereof
a little part of the flower is unpaved
the walls and partition within wantes whitinge one seate is wanting & the
glaswindowes want mendinge

The Church is unwhited and not beawtified
the windows are at defalte halfe the [floor] is unpaved
some of the seates are badd and not decent [   ]
defalte in the frame of the bells

3 November 1610

The buttrice of the south est and west corner faultie [the west end – crossed
out] the inside of the steple undecent and the healing of the porch decayed, the
west end of the north side of the Church in decay

6 December 1636

They want a new Communion ~~Tayle~~ Table & ~~a raile about it~~.
The Steeple wantes Shingling.
~~The Flower of the Church porch lyeth unpaved & very unseemly.~~
~~The Fence of the Churchyard is very ruinous & wantes reparing.~~
~~The Churchyard is much over growne with nettles & weedes.~~
There are heapes of earth & rubbish lying in the Churchyard against the
Churchwalls in a very unseemly manner.
The Floore of the North Isle of the Church is unpaved.

Boxgrove – St Mary and St Blaise

Incumbent	Patron (where known)
1602 – John Hull	Lord Lumley
1610 – John Hull	Lord Lumley
1636 – Thomas Gardner/ Samuel Hill	Sir William Morley of Halnaker

1602

(impropriator/farmer: Ralph Middleton)

The Chancel is faltie in healing
and faltie in the pavinge
and faltie in the glaswindowes

The Church is faltie in the healinge
the glaswindowes are broken and some stopped with bordes
the window in the porche is unglased
the walles on the northside are unseemely
the cover of the fonte is in two peeces

30 October 1610

The steeple unshingled the south side
ile ill slaited some of the windowes
stopped upp

25 November 1636

The Ten Commaundments and the Kings Armes want to be fairly sett up in the Church.

The Church & Chauncell want to be new whited throughout.

There are noe Sentences of Scripture sett up about the Church.

There is much Ivy groweing about the Church & Chauncell which is to be taken away.

There wantes a new Carpett for the Communion Table & another Flaggon for the Communion wyne. The Flaggon which they have is not of the Silver Fashion.

They have not a booke for the 5th of November, nor a note indented of the Utensills of the Church.

Bramber – St Nicholas   *Storrington Deanery*

Incumbent	Patron (where known)
1602 – Thomas Phipps	Magdalen College Oxford
1610 – James Wrench	
1636 – Laurence Davenport	

1602   *(impropriator/farmer: Thomas Phipps)*

The Chauncel sum what ruinous
the walles within are unwhited
the windowes unglased and it hath no seates in it

The Church hath many defectes
the roofe in the healinge
the walles within want whitinge and beawtifying
the flower is unpaved
the seates very ruinos
the Communion Table not decent
the place for the reding of publicke prayer not decent
the pulpitt wan[t]eth a deske
the fonte not decent
there is but one bell and it hangeth inconveniently in the Chauncell

3 November 1610

The buttresses of the steeple faultie & to be seeled overhead Church healinge
wanteth pointing

6 December 1636

The Communion Table Cloth is old & worne out. There wantes a new Booke of
Common Prayer. There are divers seates in the Church which want reparing.
There wantes another Flaggon for the Communion wyne. There is noe Table of
the degrees of marriage. The healing of the Church is in decay. They have noe
hoode in the Church for the Minister. The Fence of the Churchyard is very
ruinous & in decay that hogges may come through many places.

Broadwater – St Mary *Storrington Deanery*

Incumbent	Patron (where known)
1602 – Francis Heydon	
1610	
1636 – Grenado Chester	Sir Robert Chester of Herts

1602
(impropriator/farmer: Francis Heydon)

The Chauncel is very ruinous bothe in the whole roofe walles windowes and pavements

The Church is in defalte at the west ende in healinge and layinge the stoones
the northe and south dores are very ruinos and broken wantinge goodd lockes
the windowes in defect in glasinge and the Church in pavinge
the seates very uncomely and wanteth reparinge
the Church within very undecent & wanteth whitinge and bewtifyinge

3 November 1610

A buttress on the north end of the north outlett at default & the pulpett very undecent

Buncton – All Saints   *Storrington Deanery*

Incumbent   Patron (where known)

18 March 1602

The Chauncell wanteth pavinge and whitinge

The Churche hath no pulpitt, [no] font, it lackes pavinge and whitinge
the windowes are broken
it raynes in through the roofe in divers places
there are but three seates in all

6 December 1636

The Railes of the Fence of the Chappell yard are very much gone to decay &
divers pannells of the same Fence are quite downe & taken away.
The Chauncell windowe is much broken & peiced with lattice.
The Chappell windowes are likewise
broken & some partes therof are
onely lattice & not glasse.
The wall of the Chappell is so
overgrowne with ivy that it is like to
be the ruine thereof if it not be
speedily taken away.
~~John Peter the Chappell warden~~
~~appeared himself but brought not the~~
~~key of the Chappell soe that wee~~
~~Could not goe in to viewe it.~~

Burpham – St Mary   *Arundel Deanery*

Incumbent	Patron (where known)
1602 – Gregory Berrier	Dean & Chapter
1610 – Gregory Berrier	
1636 – Gregory Berrier	

1602   *(impropriator/farmer: James Marlett)*

The paving and glaswindowes neede mendinge the walles whitinge and the particions betwene the Chauncell and the Churche needeth to be repayred

The coveringe glaswindowes and pavinge need mendinge
the walles whitinge
the seates have neede to be repaired and plancked in the bottom
there wanteth allso a convenient pulpitt

11 November 1636

The Church & Chauncell want to be all new whited & beautified with Sentences of Scripture.
Many of the Seates in the Church want Boarding or paveing in the Bottoms.
There wantes a new Communion Table and a new Carpett to lay upon it.
The Assent in the Chauncell wantes to be paved.
The Byble is not of the last Translacion, nor the Communion Booke of the last edicion.
They have not the Booke of Homilies nor the Booke of Canons nor the Service Booke for the 5th of November.
There is noe note indented of the Utensills of the Church, nor Chest for Alms for the poore.
There wantes another Flaggon for the Communion wyne.
There wantes a new cloth & Carpett for the Communion Table, and a new Cloth and Cushion for the Pulpett.

Burton – St Richard   *Midhurst Deanery*

Incumbent	Patron (where known)
1602 – Henry Duppa	Sir Henry Goring
1610 – Henry Duppa	
1636 – Christopher Elderfield	Baron William Goring

25 November 1636

There are noe Sentences of Scripture Nor the Ten Commaundments nor the
Kings Armes sett up in the Church.

They want a beere in the Church.

They have noe Chest wherein to keepe the ornaments of the Church..

They want a service Booke for the 5th of November.

Bury – St John the Evangelist   *Arundel Deanery*

Incumbent	Patron (where known)
1602 – Thomas Scarborough	Bishop of Chichester
1610 – Thomas Scarborough	
1636 – John Ford	Crown

1602   *(impropriator/farmer: Richard Buttery)*

The Chauncell hath in it divers drippes

The roofe of the Churche is suncke from the steeple to the great danger of the Churche and Chauncell
the walles want whitinge and in some places plasteringe
the place for the reading of prayer is not decent
the ascent unto the pulpitt is unseemly.
The paving is broken
divers seates are faltie in the timber worke others lye under foote undecent
the porch is to be amended in the coveringe

30 October 1610

The Church porch & communion table falty

11 November 1636

There is no Cloth for the Pulpett, nor a note indented of the utensills of the Church, ~~nor a hood for the Minister.~~
The Carpett for the Communion Table is very homely & unfitting.
There wantes another Flaggon for the Communion wyne.

There is a drincking kept in the Chauncell every yeare at Easter, which they intend to continue, until they receyve Commaundment to the contrary.

~~Mr Higgons his Fence against the Churchyard wantes to be paled or rayled or walled.~~

The Cushion for the Pulpett is very badd.

The Chauncell wantes great reparcions in the Roofe therof, alsoe it wantes whiteing & beautifying with Sentences of Scripture.

There is noe Booke for the 5th of November, nor the Booke of homilies.

Chidham – St Mary   *Boxgrove Deanery*

Incumbent	Patron (where known)
1602 – William Derrick	Bishop of Chichester
1610 – William Derrick	
1636 – Robert Ball	

1602   *(impropriator/farmer: Roger Michell)*

The Chauncell pavinge is broken upp
the healing in defalte and the stoone wall
beinge the gable ende of the saide Chauncel
is to be taken upp and new made

The Churche wanteth pavinge the seates
planckinge and the belfry planckinge
windowes glasinge
the steeple to be new builded and the porche
to be walled and borded and the healinge and walles within to be amended

22 October 1610

The Church and steeple in decay and so is the Church porch

25 November 1636

The Church & Chauncell want to be all new whited & beautified & adorned
with Sentences of Scripture. ~~The Seates in the Church generally want reparing~~.
There wantes a new Pulpett Cushion.
The pavement of the Chauncell is suncke in
many places, also the Chauncell is unpaved
in many places.
There wantes a new Communion Table.
The Steeple wantes to be new boarded. ~~They
have not the Booke for the 5th of November,
not the Booke of homilies, nor the Booke of
Canons.~~
The seats in the Chauncell are much ruinated.
There is no note indented of the Utensills in the Church.
There wantes a new Seate for the Minister.
All the Southside of the Churchyard wantes fencing with railes or pales.
The steeple is like to fall down.
The North Isle of the Church wantes to be better covered and the walls want
plastring in many places. The Font wantes a new cover.
~~The monument of Henry Bickley Esq is much decaied~~ & defaced.
There wantes a new Flaggon for the Communion wyne.

Chilgrove   *Boxgrove Deanery*

Incumbent   Patron (where known)

1602   *(impropriator/farmer: Richard Storye)*

The Chauncell is at falte both in walles and roofe like to fall downe

The Church wanteth pavinge and glasse

Chithurst – (no known dedication)   *Midhurst Deanery*

Incumbent   Patron (where known)

1602
                                        (impropriator/farmer: John Packe)

The Chauncell walles glaswindowes flower and north doore at reparacions

The healinge glasinge seates and sla[ts?] are at defalte
the walles untrimed
the communion table insufficient there is no bell
the porche is at reparacions

3 November 1610

the shingle of the chapell of Chithurst in decay the glass windowes faultie &
the font there undecent

25 November 1636

The Chauncel wantes reparing in the Covering & whiteing.
There wantes a new Pulpett & Seat for the Minister.
The Ten Commaundments ~~& the Kings Armes are to be fairly sett up in the Church~~.
The Seates in the Church want reparing in every place.
The Chauncell wantes paveing.
There are noe Bells in the Church.
Noe hood for the Minister, nor Cushion nor Cloth for the Pulpett.
They have not the Service Booke for the 5th of November.
They have not the Booke of homilies.
The Church wantes reparacions generally throughout.
They have noe note indented of the utensills of the Church.

Clapham – St Mary   *Arundel Deanery*

Incumbent	Patron (where known)
1602 – David Evans	Crown
1610 – David English	
1636 – Henry Nye	Sir Thomas Holland

18 March 1603   *(impropriator/farmer: David Evans)*

The coveringe glaswindowes and paving have need to be amended and the walles new whited

The coveringe of the Churche needeth mendinge the walles whitinge the seates repairinge & planckinge in the bottom

the pavinge as decayed in sundrie places

the glaswindowes mendinge

ther wants a decent pulpitt and a communion table

the fonte allso wanteth repairinge

30 October 1610

The steeple faultie in shingle

11 November 1636

~~The Church & Chauncell want both to be new whited & adorned with Sentences of Scripture.~~

~~The place where Communion Table standeth wantes to be paved.~~

~~The twoe Seates in the Chauncell wante paveing or boarding in the Bottomes.~~

~~The Chauncell wantes paveing almost over all.~~

There is not the Booke for the 5th of November.

Their Bible is not of the last Translacion.

The Carpett for the Communion Table is linsey Woolsey & very homely & unseemly. The Cloth & Cushion for the Pulpett are the lyke.

~~There wantes a bigger Flaggon for the Communion wyne~~.

There is noe note indented of the Utensills of the Church.

Climping – St Mary   *Arundel Deanery*

Incumbent	Patron (where known)
1602 – Thomas Emerson	Crown
1610 – Thomas Emerson	
1636 – John White	Eton College

1602   *(impropriator/farmer: Edward Penfold)*

The selinge is to be mended the covering to be mended
the grounde is unpaved and to be whited

The ministers seate is to be made higher and more decent
some seates are to be repared
some places want coveringe some places want pavinge
one of the belles are broken
the rayne water runneth in to the Churche through the doors
the floore is to be made levell

30 October 1610

To certify defects & repair

25 November 1636

All the Northside of the Churchyard wantes fencing.
There wantes a new Carpett for the Communion Table & a Cloth and Cushion
for the Pulpett.
There are some Seates in the Church which want paveing.
There is noe hood for the Minister nor Table of the degrees of marriage.
Both Church & Chauncell want healing in divers places.
The Church porch wantes to be paved.
There wantes a new dore to the Belfry, the Minister saith that by reason of the
weakenesse of the old dore the Church hath bin like to have bin broken up.
There wantes a new Gate on the West side of the Churchyard.
Twoe windowes at the West end of the Church are stopped up to save
glaceing.

Coates – St Agatha   *Midhurst Deanery*

Incumbent	Patron (where known)

1602

The Chauncell lacketh some pavinge glasinge heling & whitinge

The Church porch leaneth of one side
the Churche lacketh healinge
there lacketh a seate to be made on the southeside and the doore to be made
new and wanteth some glasinge

25 November 1636

The Church porch is to be paved and the Flower to be raised a little higher.
There be are not the Ten Commaundments or other Sentences of Scripture are not sett up upon the walls of the Church.
The Mothers names of the Children are not sett downe in the Register Booke as well as the Fathers names.
They want the service Booke for the 5th of November.
Theire Church Bible is defective & is not the last Translacion.
Theire Book of Common praier is also defective & is not according to the Canon.
They have not a note indented of those things which belonge to the Church.
They have noe Chest for Almes for the poore neither a Cushion for the Pulpett.

Cocking – St Catherine of Siena   *Midhurst Deanery*

Incumbent	Patron (where known)
1602 – Henry Blaxton	Bishop of Chichester
1610 – William Mattock	
1636 – John Napper	

18 March 1602   *(impropriator/farmer: Dr Blaxton)*

The Chauncell wanteth healinge in divers places
it hathe great neede to be wasshed
the parsons seate in the Chauncell is at falte
the Chauncell doore wantes a locke and the windowes are at defalte

The Church one the southeside unpaved
in some of the seates the pavinge is decayed
xii seates at falte for wante of backes
the ministers seat is to narrow and unseemely
the pulpitt standeth inconveniently
one windowe is unglased ii windowes want repairing
the loftes in the steeple are decayed
the staires to the upper lofte be rotton
the bells cannott be runge for want of a better frame
the farmores seate standes inconveniently betwene the waye to the Chauncell

25 November 1636

The North side of the Churchyard wantes better fencing.
The Church walls want some whiteing & the Ten Commaundments ~~& the Kings Armes are quite worne out.~~
There wantes a new seate for the Minister.
Noe note indented of the utensills of the Church.
The Chauncell walls want whiteing with the Sentences of the Scripture to be sett up.
There is no Beere to carry the dead to Church.
The Challice for the Communion wyne is too little & there wantes a new Flaggon that which they have is like an Alehouse pott.

Coldwaltham – St Giles   *Midhurst Deanery*

Incumbent	Patron (where known)
1602 – William Pers	
1610 – Thomas Scarborough	
1636	

1602

The Chauncell lacketh some glasinge paving & mending of the seates and mendinge above where it hathe bin sealed

The particion cominge into the Churche to be flowred and better healed
a falte in the wall at the wast ende thereof
the Church is not whited it lacketh paving
the seates lacke to be plancked

4 November 1610

The north side of the Church wanteth pointing a rafter on the south side unsounde no reading pulpitt the plancks are faultie

December 1636

~~The Churchyard wantes all to be new railed & fenced.~~
~~There are seats in the Chauncell standing in equall height with the Communion Table.~~
The Ten Commandments are to be new sett up.
They have not a note indented in parchment of the utensills of the Church.
The Pulpett standes in the Chauncell which ought to stand in the body of the Church.

Compton – St Mary   ***Boxgrove Deanery***

Incumbent	Patron (where known)
Compton with Upmarden	
1602 – Richard Barwick	Lord Montague & Roger Bringborne
1610 – Richard Barwick	Lord Montague & Roger Bringborne
1636 – Anthony Gray	Thomas Gray of Woolbeding

1602   *(impropriator/farmer: Richard Barwick)*

The Chancell unpaved

The communion table undecent
the Churche wanteth pavinge and the fonte reparacions.

22 October 1610

The communion table undecent and the Font not decently covered

[November] 1636

All the Westend of the Churchyard wantes to be railed or paled.
The Church porch wantes paving and silling.
The Church throughout wantes to be paved & all the seats to be boarded or planked.
The reading place & the pulpett are not uniforme, & also they stand soe weakly that the Minister cannot stand steddy in either of them.
The Church & Chauncell want to be all new whited & beautified with the sentences of scripture and the Kings Arms are to be fairly sett up in the Church

The Chauncell wantes to be new paved throughout & the Seals there are very ruynous

The wyndowes in the Chauncell are dammed up to save glaseing.

The Roofe of the Chauncell wantes Covering.

They want a new Service Booke the old being old all torne.

There is noe hoode for the Minister, Nor Chest for Almes for the poore.

They have not the Booke for the 5th November, nor the Table of the Degrees of marriage, nor note indented of the utensills of the Church.

There is no Beare for to carry the dead to Church to buriale

There is noe Carpett for the Communion Table, nor chest for Almes for the poore.

All the Seates in the Church are very ruynous & many of them want silling.

There wantes a new Cover for the Font also it wantes whiting.

The Stocke of the great bell is broken.

There is a great cracke in the wall at the west end of the Church.

There is no Ascent to the Pulpett.

There is Ivy which groweth through the roofe of the Chauncell which ought to be taken away.

The Beare which is like a ladder standeth equall with the Communion Table.

There wantes a new Surplace & a new Flaggon for the Communion Wyne the old one being a wyne pott.

Coombes – (no known dedication)   *Storrington Deanery*

Incumbent	Patron (where known)
1602 – Christopher Minshull	The Shelley family
1610 – Christopher Minshull	
1636 – John Eliot	Sir John Shelley

1602   *(impropriator/farmer: C Minshull)*

The Chauncel wanteth whitinge within and [in] one place unpaved
the glasse broken
the dore going out in to the Churchyearde is not very good & the seates want a
littell repayringe

The Churche needethe whitinge & is not bewtified
the seates are out of order
the glasse windowes lacke mendinge
it hath but one bel and the steeple is a littell faltie in one place of the healinge

3 November 1610

The healing of the Church wanteth pointing, the belfrie verie undecent, the
steeple crackt in the wall

6 December 1636

~~The Communion Table is not railed in.~~ They want a new Carpett for the
Communion Table. ~~Some of the Seates in the body of the Church want
boarding in the bottome.~~
~~They use to sett a bason in the Font to hold water for Baptismes.~~
There are some defectes in the healing of the Church.
~~The Fence of the Churchyard wantes amending in divers places.~~
~~They have noe hood for the Minister.~~
~~They have noe Table of the degrees of marriage.~~

Didling – St Andrew *Midhurst Deanery*

Incumbent	Patron (where known)
1602 – Hugh Rawood	
1610 – Thomas Price	
1636 – Nathaniel White	

1602 *(impropriator/farmer: Thos Blackman)*

The Chauncell wantes ridge tilles the walles morteringe and washinge
the flower unpaved
~~the communion table decayed~~
~~the seates decayed~~
the oves unstopt
the partition betwene the Chauncell and the Church is open

The Church wantes healinge
the cheast for the regester boocke and other implements of the Church is in
peeces without lockes or keyes or cover
the oves of the Churche is open
the seates unplancked
the Church unpaved
the fonte uncovered
the seates that shoulde be in the south side of the Churche cleane taken awaye
the windows are in falte
the walles without wantes reparinge
the communion table is decayed
the seates in the Chauncell are decayed

25 November 1636

The Church porch wantes reparing in the Pavement & healing thereof.
The Communion Table is not railed about & doth not stand north and South.
The Chauncell walls want plaistering & whiteing.
The Pavement in the midle Isle of the Church is suncke.

There is neither Bible, Communion Booke, Booke of homilies, booke of Canons, Service Booke for the 5th of November, Flaggon nor Challice for the Communion wyne, nor Carpett for the Communion Table nor hood for the Minister, Cloth nor Cushion for the Pulpett nor chest for the Register Booke nor Chest for Almes for the Poore in the Church.

The Seates in the Chauncell rancke themselves with the Communion Table on both sides.

The Church wantes reparing in the Covering in many places.

Donnington – St George   *Boxgrove Deanery*

Incumbent	Patron (where known)
1602 – Thomas Harrison	Bishop of Chichester
1610 – Thomas Harrison	
1636 – George Edgley	

18 March 1602   *(impropriator/farmer: George Arderne & R Middleton)*
The Chauncell rough wanteth shingles
the wainscott sealinge overheade is rotten and decayed
the pavement in divers places broken
the seates are not stronge nor decent
the walles in some places begin to mulder downe & want whitinge

The Church roofe is full of drippes
the Churche is not all paved
the flower is muche brocken
the seates are most of them in muche decay & the flower very roughe
the walles begin to mulder downe
the fonte wold have a decent coveringe
a chappell of the Church hath the pavement much brocken
the stones in the windows are much broken and the window like to fall downe
the two doores are in muche decaye
and some of the sealinge fallen
downe by reason of a drippe and
some parte of the wall thereof doe
mulder downe
the steeple speere is not well covered
& the windowe holes of the steeple
stand allwayes open to all weather
very hurtful to the timber worke of
the [belfry?]

22 October 1610

There is no preaching pulpett

[November] 1636

To see the Churchyard sufficiently fenced;
to provide a neue surplice for the Minister;
to provide a chest for alms for the poore;
to provide a better cloth and cussion for the pulpett;
to new white the Church,
to remove the dunghills now behind the Church porch,
to provide A larger Clothe for the Communion Table;
~~there is a Timber in~~ the healin the Chancel in the north side of the Communion
table and make [?] to repar the font where it wantes mendinge;
the belfrie wantes paving and the windowes glased;
to see the decaies of the steple suffic[iently] roped;
to present the decaies of the Chauncelle.

Duncton – St Mary   *Midhurst Deanery*

Incumbent	Patron (where known)
1602 – John Taylor	
1610 – John Street	
1636 – David German	

1602

The Chancel lacketh to be whited and beter glassed

The Church porche to be stripped [on] the northside
the Church to be whited and the seates to be planked
the northside of the Church to be better tyled

25 November 1636

There wantes a new Communion Table.
The Seates in the Chauncell wantes boarding & some of these seates stand
equall with the Communion Table & are to be taken away.
The Chauncell wantes to be beautified with Sentences of Scripture.
The Bible is not of the last Translacion.
They want the Service Booke for the 5th of November.
There is noe Cloth for the Pulpett.
They have noe note indented of the Utensills of the Church.
Robert Pannell & Richard Yeldall doe not pay the Clark his wages.
There wantes a new Flaggon for the Communion wyne.

Earnley – (no known dedication)   *Boxgrove Deanery*

Incumbent	Patron (where known)
1602 – Laurence Bond	Crown
1610 – Henry Warner	Bishop of Chichester
1636 – Edmund Ryshton	George Ryshton

1602   *(impropriator/farmer: Elinor Weston)*

The Chauncell is not paved
the walles want whitinge
the upper parte betweene of the particion betweene the Churche wolde be new
plastered and whited

The west ende of the Churche is not paved
the south doore wanteth locke and keye
the northwest ende hathe a littell broken window in the one side
the toope of the steeple wanteth a cocke

22 October 1610

The Church wanteth light in the west end

[November] 1636

To provide A bible of the last translation, the book of homilies; to provide a
cover to the pulpett; A table of the digrees of marriage; A note indented of the
utensels of the Church; A better Carpett for the communion table and A new
surplis; And A new communion [book[of the last edition.

Eartham – St Margaret   *Boxgrove Deanery*

Incumbent	Patron (where known)
1602 – Ralph Earle	Thomas Goodall
1610 – Ralph Earle	
1636 – Michael Glyd	Richard Lewkenor

1602 [badly torn at top]   *(impropriator/farmer: Ralph Earle)*

The Chauncell is falte with healinge and in the pavement
The Church is in decaye in healinge
the walles unseemely
the glass windowes faltie,
the pavement is not well
the seates want mending
the porch is faltie
one of the bells are in defalte
the font will hold no water
the ministers seat is unseemly
the south doore is not sufficient

22 October 1610

The porch and Church ill covered the pulpett and communion table verie undecent

25 November 1636

The Church Porch wantes silling.
Both Church & Chauncell want much reparing in the healing.
The Church & Chauncell want all to be new whited & adorned with Sentences
of Scripture and the Kings Arms.
Here wantes a new suplace for the Minister.
The Chauncell wantes paveing in many places.
There wantes a new hood for the Minister.
They have not a note indented of the Utensills of the Church.
There is a seat in the Chauncell which wantes plancking.
Divers Seates in the Church want boarding or paveing.
The Font will not hold water they christen in a bason.
There is noe Flaggon for the Communion wyne.

Easebourne – St Mary   *Midhurst Deanery*

Incumbent	Patron (where known)
1602 – Thomas Tyse	
1610 – Constantine Harman	
1636 – John Allenson	Crown

1602   *(impropriator/farmer: George Dennis)*

The Chauncell south and east walles at reparacions
the glas windowes, paving, seates and north dore at reparacions

The healinge on the south ile at some defecte
the communion table not sufficient
the walles glass windowes pavinge and west dore at reparacions
vii or viii of the seates to be repaired the residew very undecent for want of
flowering
the Church porche unclosed

30 October 1610

The Church in decay in healinge

11 November 1636

They have not the service Booke for the 5th of November.
~~There is a Seate on the East side of the Chauncell which ranckes equall with the
Communion Table.~~
~~The Chauncell wantes beautifying with Sentences of Scripture.~~
They want a Cushion for the Pulpett.
They have not a note indented of the utensills of the Church.
They want another Flaggon for the Communion wyne.
The pavement at the lower end of the Chauncell is suncke in some parts thereof.
The Font if it be removed from the South Side of the Church where it standes
inconveniently & set neere to the North dore of the Church it will gain roome
enough for 30 or 40 persons to sit & hear divine Service and sermons. There
being as the Font standeth not roome enough to receyve them all.
All the East end of the South Isle of the Church is soe much given to decay that
if it be not speedily amended yt will certenly fall downe.

East Dean – All Saints   *Boxgrove Deanery*

Incumbent	Patron (where known)
1602 – John Chaplin	John Large & Thomas Brabon
1610 – William Wilson	
1636 – Richard Halsey	Robert Garton

1602   *(impropriator/farmer: Thos Heberden)*

[badly torn at the top of a page]
the communion table not decent ....
windowes want mendinge
there are no [seats?]

the Church wanteth pavinge between the [pace?] and seates
some seates want mendinge
the windowes want glasing
the ministers seate is undecent
the south dore is at falte wanteth a locke
The communion table not decent

22 October 1610

A buttress of the Church in decay
there wanteth a pulpett, and the porch
much decayed
and the Church in decay in covering

25 November 1636

All the Southside of the Churchyard
wantes railing or paling.
There are divers dunghills in the
Churchyard.
The Church porch wantes paveing or cilling.

The Church wantes whiteing & to be adorned with Sentences of Scripture & the Kings Armes are to be fairly sett up in the Church.

The Church wantes paveing in many places.

There wantes a new Communion Table.

There are divers seates in the Church which want plancking or boarding.

The Chauncell wantes to be all new ~~whited~~ covered. Also it wantes to be whited in the side & to be paved.

There wantes a better Carpett for the Communion Table and a new Cloth & Cushion for the Pulpett.

There is no Booke of homilies, nor Booke of Cannons, neither the Booke for the 5th of November.

There is noe Flaggon for the Communion wyne nor hoode for the Minister.

There is noe Chest for Almes for the Poore, Nor for the Register Booke.

They have noe note indented of the utensills of the Church.

The Seates in the Church are not uniforme.

The Chauncell windows want glaceing.

East Marden – St Peter   *Boxgrove Deanery*

Incumbent	Patron (where known)
1602 – Edmund Orson	Elizabeth Benion
1610 – William Heaton	
1636 – William Chambers	Elizabeth Baylie

1602   *(impropriator/farmer: Edmund Orson)*

The Chauncel is unpaved & the windowes want glasinge

The Church is unpaved

22 October 1610

~~The Church wanteth light~~

The Church porch very badd

East Preston – St Mary   *Arundel Deanery*

Incumbent	Patron (where known)
1602 – Lawrence Alcock	Crown
1610	
1636 – Humphrey Streete	

1602   *(impropriator/farmer: Richard Snelling)*

The covering paving the windowes & seates are to be repaired
the walls to be whited

The seates are all ruinos and have neede to be all new made & plancked in the bottome
the glas windows & paving of the chappel neede mendinge and the covering of the chappel and porch
the north doore and the stoone works over that and the south dore have neede to be repaired
the stoneworke of the steeple & the frame of the belles neede mending & a decent table for the communion is wanting

30 October 1610

The Church wanteth light & a howse standinge in the Church yard in decay which should be repaired by the parishioners

11 November 1636

The Churchyard wantes fencing on all partes.
The Church porch wantes paveing.
~~There wantes a new Pulpett to be sett in a more convenient place~~.
The Chauncell wantes whiteing and Sentences of the Scripture.
The wyndowes in the Chauncell want glaceing.
There is noe Table of the degrees of marriage, Nor Booke of homilies, nor Service Booke for the 5th of November.
Noe note indented of the utensills of the Church.
Nor Chest for Almes for the poore.
There wantes a Carpett for the Communion Table & a cloth and Cushion for the Pulpett.

East Wittering – Assumption of St Mary the Virgin   *Boxgrove Deanery*

Incumbent	Patron (where known)
1602 – Samuel Todd	Bishop of Chichester
1610 – Samuel Todd	
1636 – Richard Austin	

18 March 1602   *(impropriator/farmer: Samuel Todd)*

The Chauncell wanteth pavinge
the sealing is altogether ruinous
the windowes overgronne with mosse and canker and there wanteth tilinge

The communion table hath a badd frame covered with a course plancke
the communion cloth is very badd
the Church not at all paved
the seates are very broke and the flower very badd
the windowes are to fewe & very darke
the particion between the Chauncell and it wanteth plastering
the font wanteth a good cover
the north doore is not hanged up and wanteth a locke and keye
there is no 2d pulpitt to preache in
ther is no belfrye the ii bells hange outwardly at the west ende
the porche wanteth bordes one bothe sides

22 October 1610

The buttress of the Church in decay

[November] 1636

To ~~see the~~ present the seates in the Chauncell are not sufficiently repared and
the Chauncell new whited to ~~pave~~ the place where the Communion table
stands; to provide A Cushion for the pulpett; there wantes A new Communion
table

Eastergate –St George

Incumbent	Patron (where known)
1602 – Godfrey Blaxton	Dean & Chapter
1610 – Godfrey Blaxton	
1636 – Augustine Payne	

1602
(impropriator/farmer: Godfrey Blaxton)

In the Chauncell the glasse windows are to be amended

the pargitinge in the East is to be repaired and the walles to be whited

the tile and Horsham stone to be new layed and pointed and the roofe is to be made close

In the Churche there is but one (and that unseemely) seate for the minister to read prayers & to preach in which would [be rendered?] higher and made larger

many places are unpaved and some places paved neede to be made levell

the walles need whiting & the tenn commandementes to be new written.

All the covering to be new layed and pointed the ovis to be made close

most of the seates are unseemely and all of them neither paved nor plancked

there needeth a new cover for the fonte

30 October 1610

The Church verie ill covered

25 November 1636

The Church wantes to be all new whited & the Tenn Commaundements & the Kinges Armes are quite worne out.

There wantes a new Cover for the Font.

The Chauncell wantes to be new whited & beawtified with Sentences of Scripture.

There is noe Booke for the 5th of November nor note indented of the Utensills of the Church.

The Bible is not of the last Translacion.

There is noe Cloth nor Cushion for the Pulpett nor Carpett for the Communion Table nor Table of the degrees of marriage.

The Surplace is very unseemely & not fitting for the Minister.

Egdean – St Bartholomew   *Midhurst Deanery*

Incumbent	Patron (where known)
1602	
1610	
1636 – Ralph Blinston	Crown

11 November 1636

~~The Communion Table is not railed in.~~

They want a Flaggon for the Communion wyne.

They want the Booke of Cannons & ~~a Register booke.~~

The walls at the west end of the Church want plaistring & are very unseemly.

They have noe Carpett for the Communion Table.

The Ten Commaundments are not sett up in the Church nor any Sentences of Scripture.

Elsted – St Paul   *Midhurst Deanery*

Incumbent	Patron (where known)
1602 – John Wynne	Thomas Hanbury
1610 – John Wynne	
1636 – John Knigh	Crown

1602   *(impropriator/farmer: John Winne)*

The Chauncell wantes shingles
the glass windowes want mendinge

The Church wantes wasshinge the seates are unplancked
the windowes are in defalte it rayneth into the Church through the steeple
the roofe wantes mendinge the communion table is unseemely
there wanteth a cloth to hang over the pulpitt & a better surplishe
we want a decent cloth to cover the communion table

30 October 1610

The Church in great decay in healinge, in the buttresses & wall the wall wants
coatinge on the south side the communion table undecent the Church porch in
decay the rafters in the north wall verie rotten and there wanteth light

25 November 1636

The Church wantes shingling in many places.
There wantes a new Pulpett; That which is there already is too lowe and not
uniforme.
The Seates in the Chauncell are much decayed.
The Church wantes to be beautified with Sentences of Scripture.
The Ten Commaundments & the Kings Armes which are sett up in the Church
are very dymm & almost worne out.
The Churchyard is not kept sweet & cleane but is full of rubbysh.
There is neither Cloth nor Cushion for the Pulpett.
They have not the Service Booke for the 5th of November. Nor note indented of
the utensills of the Church.

Felpham – St Mary   *Arundel Deanery*

Incumbent	Patron (where known)
1602 – Garrett Williamson	Dean & Chapter
1610 – William Cox	Richard Perrin by grant Dean & Chpt
1636 – Thomas Boxall	Sarah Cox, widow of Wm

1602   *(impropriator/farmer: Alban Stoughton)*

    There to be repared the tylinge
    the seatinge needes some reparacion
    the walles are not well whited
    the ovis under the roofe is to be made close

    Some falte in the tilinge
    a new pulpit to be placed in a more convenient rome
    the timber worke in the steeple is to be repared
    the ovis to be made close
    some seates to be made more decent some want paving

30 October 1610

    The porch of the Church at default in coveringe & a windowe of the Church
    unglaced & the communion table undecent

6 December 1636

    The Church porch wantes paveing.
    The Chauncell is not adorned with
    Sentences of Scripture, it being to be
    done by Mr Cox.
    There is a Seate in the Chauncell which
    wantes boarding or paveing.
    There is not the Booke for the 5th of
    November.
    There wantes a bigger Flaggon for the Communion wyne.

There is noe hood for the Minister.

The Chauncell wantes paveing in many places.

They have not a note indented of the Utensills of the Church.

The Church wantes whiteing & beautifying with the Kinges Armes & Sentences of Scripture.

The dore at the Eastend of the Church wantes much reparing.

There are some seates in the Church next to the Chauncell which want boarding.

Fernhurst – St Margaret of Antioch   *Midhurst Deanery*

Incumbent	Patron (where known)
1602 – Hugh Jones	
1610 – John Bennett	
1636 – John Bennett	

1602   *(impropriator/farmer: Thos Farnden)*

ii buttresses in the outside northe Chauncell wall at defect
the pavinge and seates likewise at defecte

The Church in healinge wanteth closinge
the seates want mendinge and floweringe
the pavinge walles west doore and Church porche at defecte

30 October 1610

The Church and porch in decay & the steple crackt in the wall

Ferring – St Andrew   *Arundel Deanery*

Incumbent	Patron (where known)
1602 – Peter Walters	Prebendary of Ferring
1610 – John Bell	
1636 – Arthur Owen	

1602   *(impropriator/farmer: Richard Snelling)*

The Chauncell is all unpaved the seates decayed
the walles need whiting and the glass windowes need covering & mending

The seates are all ruinos & unplancked on the bottom
the walles neede whitinge
the glas windowes and pavinge mendinge especially the north isle is all
unpaved & the windowe next the ministers seate wolde be ~~mended~~ and made
light
the font sett somewhat hier and the stoneworke about it to be amended
there is no steeple the belles hange in a frame in the Church yard

30 October 1610

To certify defects & repair

11 November 1636

There wantes another Flaggon for the Communion wyne, and a new Carpett
for the Communion Table & a Cover for the Pulpett.
There are twoe Seates in the Chauncell which are very ruynous & want
reparing.
The Lower end of the Church wantes paveing.
There is noe note indented of the utensills of the Church.
The Chauncell wantes adorning with Sentences of Scripture.
The Churchyard wantes fencing on all partes.

Findon – St John   *Storrington Deanery*

Incumbent	Patron (where known)
1602 – George Simpson	Magdalen College, Oxford
1610 – Richard Bowghton	
1636 – Toby Harcke alias Garbrande	

1602   *(impropriator/farmer: Thos Whatman)*

The Chauncell is very ruinos in the whole rofe
the windows muche broken and unglased
the pavementes broken
the partition gutter between the parsons Chauncell and the Chauncell as they
call it is in greate defalte and the walls and timber worke through the same
much decayed

There wanteth a decent and sufficient communion table
the font not decent
the Church there in all partes of the rofe very ruinous both in the stone and
timber beinge ready to fall
the windowes in great defalte of glasinge and the whole Church of paving.
The seates very ruinous and Church porch within is very unseemely

3 November 1610
The timber of the steeple faultie

6 December 1636

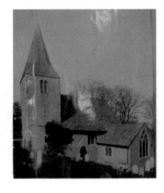

~~There wantes a new larger~~[stet]~~Carpett for the
Communion Table.~~
~~There wantes~~[stet]~~a faire larger Flaggon for the
Communion wyne.~~
The Chauncell walls want whiteing in th'nside.
~~The healing of the Church wantes poynting.~~

Fittleworth – St Mary   *Midhurst Deanery*

Incumbent	Patron (where known)
1602 – Arthur Howsden	Crown
1610 – Christopher Green	Bishop of Chichester
1636 – William Hind	

1602   *(impropriator/farmer: Arthur Howsden)*

The Chauncell lacketh healinge some pavinge
there are crackes in the wall on the east side
the doore to be mended one the southside for cominge in of piggeons

The Churche wanteth whitinge & pavinge
the seates must be plancked
there is a cracke [gon] in a walle goinge into the Chancell
the Churche of the southside must be stripte the steeple repaired and a
window over the northside mended

4 November 1610

The communion table undecent

11 November 1636

One of the ~~Pannells of pales of the Churchyard neere the Churchyard gate~~
~~wantes reparing.~~
~~The Steeple wantes shingling.~~
~~Noe Sentences of Scripture in the Chauncell.~~
~~They wantes a bigger Flaggon to Consecreate the Communion wyne.~~
They have noe note indented of the utensills of the Church.
They have noe Chest for Almes for the Poore.
There are twoe Seates at the South dore of the Church which are very
unseemly.
There wantes a surplice.

Ford – St Andrew   *Arundel Deanery*

Incumbent	Patron (where known)
1602 – John Ellis	Crown
1610 – John Ellis	Crown
1636 – John Marshall	Bishop of Chichester

1602   *(impropriator/farmer: John Ellis)*

The tilinge is to be ~~new repaired~~ the walles to be whited and the seates to be mended

The walles are to be whited
some places to be paved
the fonte to be amended
the seates to be new bilte the olde are unseemly
a decent waye to gett upp to the steeple

30 October 1610

The Church wall crackt & the porch ill covered & the posts verie rotten

25 November 1636

There wantes a Cover for the ~~Font~~ Pulpett & the Booke of homilies & the Booke for the 5th of November.
There is noe Table of the degrees of marriage.
The Church Porch is not paved at all.
There wantes a new Cover for the Font.
There wantes a stronge & sufficient ladder to goe up into the Belfry.
There wantes a new Carpett & lynnen for the Communion Table.
The Surplace is not large enough.
There is a grave or twoe suncke in the Chauncell.
There is noe note indented of the utensills of the Church.
The Font will not hold water.
There wantes a Sadder Coloured Cloth & Cushion for the Pulpett; those which they have are very unseemley & insufficient.
The Churchyard wantes fenceing almost in every part thereof.
Theire Flaggon for the Communion wyne is like an Alehouse pott.

Funtington – St Andrew   *Boxgrove Deanery*

Incumbent	Patron (where known)
1602 – Thomas Frankwell	Dean & Chapter
1610 – Robert Tayer	
1636	

1602   *(impropriator/farmer: William Kember)*

The Chauncell is very ruinos the walles readdie to fall downe the rofe uncovered and in some places the timber rotten and the pavement full of holles and the glasse windowes decayed

The Churche seates are undecent not [borded] nor paved
the flower is not sufficient
the windows unglased
the steeple walles decayed & the Church like to goe to ruen for want of coveringe

22 October 1610

The Church in decay in divers places & wanteth light

25 November 1636

The Church & Chauncell want to be all new whited & beawtifyed with sentences of scripture.
~~The Seates in the Chauncell ranke them selves with the Communion Table on both sides.~~
There wantes a better Carpett for the Communion Table.
There is no note indented of the utensills in the Church.
The Chauncell wantes Covering.

There is a Cracke at the upper end of the Chauncell wall which if it be not speedily amended will fall downe.

There wantes an other flaggon for the Communion wyne, and a better pulpet cloth.

The seates in the Church are not sufficient to conteyne the parrishioners. But yf they were set closer together they would be large enough to receave them.

The Chauncell wantes to be paved & better levelled.

~~There wantes a new Cover for the Font.~~

The North end of the Churchyard wantes to be all new fenced.

Goring – St Mary   *Storrington Deanery*

Incumbent	Patron (where known)
1602 – John Mustion	
1610 – William Smith	Edward Michell
1636 – Robert D'Oyley	Nathaniel Weston of London

1602   *(impropriator/farmer: Thos Cooke)*
The Chauncel wanteth sealinge over as heretofore it hath bin
there wanteth a dore to a rome called the vestrie at the ende of the Chauncel
the windows in defect in glasinge
the walls and partitions within are not bewtified with sentences of scripture

The Church in the whole rofe is in defalte of poyntinge & in some part is now layringe the stones
the leades and gutter between the lower and the west ende of the Churche is in greate defalte where through the same the walles and timber is gon to ruen
the steeple is indefect in shingling
the seates in the Church are not decently repaired & kept but are in greate defalte in flowering & other necessary thinges.
The walles allso within want whitinge & bewtifying with sentences of scripture

3 November 1610
Manie of the windowes stopped up wherefor the Church is darke, the shinglinge of the steeple faultie & the west porch taken cleane away

6 December 1636
They want a new Communion praier Booke. And a fairer and better Surplace for the Minister, & a better Cover for theire pulpett Cushion.
The Seates in the Chauncell want Boarding in the Bottomes.
They have noe Chest for Almes for the poore.
The Chauncell walls want whiteing in thinside.
A great part of the Flower on the North side of the Church is unpaved.
Divers of the Seates in the Church are unboarded in the bottomes.
The Ten Commaundmentes are darkenned & defaced that they Cannot be read.

Graffham – St Giles   *Midhurst Deanery*

Incumbent	Patron (where known)
1602 – John Lancaster	
1610 – William Stepneth	Crown as ward of Thomas Garton
1636 – Oliver Pennycodd	Henry Garton

1602

The Churche walles are faltie
there porche lacke roofe
the wall is overgronne with weedes
And the porche wantes reparacions healing there are none
the glasse wantethe mending
there wantethe paving
the seates are all weeke olde and ruinos
the steeple there lackes rough castinge in the south side

30 October 1610

The north porch unhealed & wanteth a reading pulpett

25 November 1636

The Sentences of Scripture sett up in the Chauncell are almost worne out.
They want a new Communion praier Booke & the Service Booke for the 5th of
November.
The Carpett for the Communion Table is very badd.
They have noe note indented in parchment of the Utensills of the Church.
They want a Flaggon of a potle for the Communion wyne.
The Ten Commaundments & the Kings Armes want to be new sett in the
Church.

Greatham – (no known dedication)   *Storrington Deanery*

Incumbent	Patron (where known)
1602 – Richard Boley	Crown
1610 – Richard Boley	
1636 – John Chaloner	Thomas Mille

1602   *(impropriator/farmer: Richard Boley)*

The Chauncell is muche in decaye
the maine wall hath breeches the windowes are all broken
parte of the roofe is uncovered
the flower unpaved

There is no pulpitt the lower parte of the Churche is unpaved
in the nether ende of the Churche there are three badd seates
the steeple is only covered with bordes & at the bottome of the same it rayneth
in much to the Churche muche by reason the roofe is unmended

3 November 1610

There wantes a preaching pulpett the copinge of the Church wall must be
mended & the Church wants light

25 November 1636

There are Seates in the Chauncell which stand equall with the Communion
Table.
There are Chests to be removed which stand close to the Communion Table.
There is noe assent to the Communion Table.
The Booke of Common praier is old & torn.
There is noe flaggon for the Communion wyne.
There is noe Table of the degrees of marriage.
The Churchporch wantes paveing.
There is noe Chest for almes for the poore.
The Register Booke is not kept in the Church.
They have not the Booke of homilies nor Canons.
The fence of the Churchyard is much in decay in many places.

Hardham – St Botolph   *Midhurst Deanery*

Incumbent	Patron (where known)
1602 – Robert Goodyer	Crown
1610	
1636 – Edmund Wellham	Crown

1602

The Chauncell lackes stripinge, glasinge, whitinge and pavinge

The Churche lacketh helinge glasinge paving whitinge a seate for the minister
the seates want planking
a new doore to be made northwood

4 November 1610

The communion table undecent there wants a reading pulpett a post in the
Church porch rotten the Church wanteth pointing

25 November 1636

The Churchyard is at default in
fencing in every part thereof.
Noe note indented of the utensills &
implementes of the Church.
They want Bell Ropes.
~~One of the bells wantes a frame & by~~
~~reason thereof it cannot be runge at~~
~~all.~~
There wantes a ladder to goe up to
the bells.

Heyshott – St James   *Midhurst Deanery*

Incumbent	Patron (where known)
1602 – John Taylor	Crown
1610	
1636 – Joseph Henshaw	

1602

Many of the seates at reparacions
the walles glas windowes pavinge and Churche porche at reparacions

30 October 1610

Wanteth a preaching pulpett, & a windowe on the north side of the Church & a cover for the font

25 November 1636

There wantes a new Communion Table.
There is noe Carpett for the Communion Table.
The Church wantes whiteing throughout.
The Chauncell wantes whiteing & the Sentences of the Scripture there are quite worne out.
The Chauncell wantes much reparing in the walls both inside & out side.
They have not the Service Booke for the 5th of November nor the Booke of Cannons.
They want another Flaggon for the Communion wyne & a more comely Surplace for the Minister.
The Church wantes paveing.
They have not a note indented in parchment of the utensills of the Church.
The North Isle of the Church wantes paveing & the walls want plaistring.
There is noe Chest for Alms for the Poore.
There are twoe Seates in the Chauncell which stand & the people sett with their Backes to the Communion Table.
They want a new Register Booke.

Horsham – St Mary   *Storrington Deanery*

Incumbent	Patron (where known)
1602 – Matthew Allen	Bishop of Chichester & Archbishop of Canterbury
1610 – Samuel Collins	Archbishop of Canterbury
1636 – John Collins	

1602   *(impropriator/farmer: John Willet)*

The glass windowes are most of them unglased and the seates in the north parte broken & tottering & the most part of them seates unplancked.
~~The steeple is in defalte for want of shingles a Chappell annexed the Chauncell in defaulte where it rayneth in.~~
The windowes in the Chauncell want glasinge.

The windows are most of them unglased and the Seates in the north parte broken and tottering & the most part of them seates unplancked.
The steeple is at default for want of shingles.

30 October 1610

The buttress of the vestrie defective the west porch wanteth pointing a cracke in the wall of steeple the healinge of the south ile faultie the buttress of the south side of the Church faultie and the buttress on the south est corner of the steeple much decayed and the font wanteth a cover

6 December 1636

The Communion Table is not yett sett at the upper end of the Chauncell neither doth it stand North & South, neither is it yett railed.
The Seates which stand round the Communion Table for the Communicantes to sitt on are not yet taken away.
They want another Flaggon for the Communion wyne.

Houghton – St Nicholas

Arundel Deanery

Incumbent	Patron (where known)

1602   *(impropriator/farmer: James Lacker)*

The Chauncell is faultie in glasinge in flowering and in the covering the walles are to be whited

There be drippes in the Churche the windowes want glasinge the walles whitinge & the pavement is to be amended the place for the readinge of common prayer is undecent the communion table is undecent

30 October 1610

The Church wanteth light

11 November 1636

The Church wantes to be beautified with Sentences of Scripture.
The ~~Chauncell wantes beautifying with Sentences of Scripture~~.
There wantes a Flaggon or a potle for the Communion wyne; the old one is a Ewer.
There is not the Service Booke for the 5th of November, nor chest for alms for the poore.

Hunston – St Leodegar   *Boxgrove Deanery*

Incumbent	Patron (where known)
1602 – Brian Lister	Thomas Bowyer
1610 – Thomas Emerson	Crown
1636 – Peter German	Thomas Bowyer

1602   *(impropriator/farmer: John Packe)*

The Chauncell is not all paved
the glas windowes very fowle
the walles are not whited

The Church is unpaved and the seates flower is much broken underfoote
the communion table wanteth a better cover
there is no 2d pulpitt to preach in
the west doore is decayed and lacketh locke and key
there is no steple at all the bells hange in frames of stone
the porche flower is to lowe & receiveth much water thereby

22 October 1610

The Church in default in coveringe there is no pulpett, a window in the west
end of the Church stopped up

25 November 1636

All the Northside & Eastend of the Churchyard wantes to be fenced either with
railes or pales.
~~The Chauncell wantes Covering in many places.~~
~~There wantes a more Convenient & fitter reading place for the Minister.~~
The Church & Chauncell want to be whited & beautified with Sentences of
Scripture.
There wantes a better Carpett for the Communion Table; the old is like an
Alehouse Carpett.

There wantes a new & more Convenient Communion Table, the old is three feete too longe.

Their Communion Booke is not of the last Edicion.

There wantes a flaggon for the Communion wyne & a better lynnen Cloth for the Communion Table.

~~There is no hood for the Minister, no~~r Table of the degrees of marriage.

There are noe Stairs to goe up into the Pulpett.

There wantes a better Cloth & Cushion for the Pulpett.

They have noe note indented of the Utensills of the Church.

There wantes a Beere to Carry the dead to Church.

The halfe pace about the font wantes paveing.

There is noe particion between the Church & the Chauncell.

The Register book is not kept in the Church but at the vicars house.

~~The Pulpett & the reading place are to be removed to the South of the Church.~~

The most of the Seates in the Church want boarding & paveing.

There wantes a new Register Book.

There are twoe or three dunghills in the Churchyard.

Iping – St Mary   *Midhurst Deanery*

Incumbent	Patron (where known)
1602 – John Packe	Thos. & Peter Betsworth
1610 – Edward Gray	
1636 – Edward Gray	Crown

1602   *(impropriator/farmer: John Packe)*

The Chauncell walles & partition
unwhited
the glasinge & paving at reparacions

The walles untrimmed
the paving broken
the seates undecent
iiii little windows unglased
i bell broken
the flower and the Church porche at reparacions

3 November 1610

The wall at the west end of the Church the shingle at the south west end and
the north side of the porch much faultie, the font crackt and the ridge of the
Church Chancel some of the rafters verie rotten, and the pulpett undecent

25 November 1636

There is a litle skilling at the South end of the Churchyard which, as Mr Gray
saith, was taken out of the Churchyard.
The Seates in the Chauncell rancke themselves with the Communion Table on
both sides.
All the Seates in the Church want paveing or boarding in the bottomes.
They want the Booke of homilies and a Service booke for the 5th of November.
The walls in the Chauncell want reparing in many places.
The Ten Commaundements & ~~the Kings Armes want to be~~ new sett up in the
Church.
The Chauncell wantes whiteing and beautifying with the Sentences of
Scripture.
The Church walls want whiteing throughout.
There wantes a new Surplace & a new Communion Booke.
There are many Tiles in the Chauncell which are to be removed.
They have not a note indented of the utensills of the Church.
The South side of the Churchyard wantes to be better fenced.

Itchingfield – St Nicholas
Storrington Deanery

Incumbent	Patron (where known)
1602 – John Pratt	Bishop of Chichester
1610 – William Pratt	
1636 – John Scull	Mary Lewkner & Martha Blount

1602 *(impropriator/farmer: John Pratt)*

The Chauncel wanteth whitinge within and a litle of pavinge

The Church is not whited & bewtified within
the flower is not paved
the pulpitt is very badd & the deske or place to read publicke [prayers]
seates some of them want mendinge

3 November 1610

The south est windowe of the Church decaied the north buttress of the Church faultie and the Church and porch unpointed

6 December 1636

~~The Communion Table is not railed in.~~
~~There are divers seates which stand in the Chauncell in equall height with the Communion Table even to the East wall of the Chauncell.~~
Divers of the seates in the body of the Church are very old & much decayed & want to be repaired.
~~The Pulpett Cloth & Cushion are very old & worne out & not fitt to be used.~~
~~The Ten Commaundmentes are not sett up at the East end of the Church or Chauncell but on the North side of the Church~~
~~The Church walls want whiteing.~~
The Pavement of the Church & ~~Chauncell~~ are much in decay & want repaireing.
The Booke of Common praier is torn & imperfect.
They want a fair Flaggon for the Communion wyne.

The Fence of the Churchyard is very badd & insufficient in many places. And on the North & East it is but a hedge having divers brackes & holes into the same.

There is A house adioyning to the Churchyard which hath a door opening ymediatly into the same.

There is no chest for Almes for the poore but that wherein the Register bookes & ornamentes are kept.

The healing of the Church is in decay in many places.

Kingston – (no known dedication)

Arundel Deanery

Incumbent	Patron (where known)
1602 – Richard Kitson	Crown
1610 – John Postlethwaite	
1636 – Thomas Jeffrey	Crown as Lord Sandys a minor

1602

(impropriator/farmer: Richard Snelling)

The Chauncell is unpaved
the seates decayed
the [.....] & coveringe need mendinge and the walles whitinge

The whole chappell is unpaved
the seates are ruinos
the coveringe greatly decayed
the glasse windowes and doores neede mendinge
the walles whitinge
they want also a bible a pulpitt and linen clothes for the communion table

30 October 1610

The communion table undecent and the chapell wanteth light

Kirdford – St John the Baptist   *Midhurst Deanery*

Incumbent	Patron (where known)
1602 – George Payne	Lord Lumley
1610 – George Payne	
1636 – John Horton	Nicholas Plummer & Elizabeth Lumley

1602   *(impropriator/farmer: John West)*

The Chauncel windowes want glasse
the pavinge is not sufficient

The Churche at reparacions in poynting
the vestrie wantes coveringe
the glasse at reparacions
the paving is not sufficient
the seates are not plancked under foote
Communion table wanteth mending

25 November 1636

The Church ~~porch~~ yard wantes to be
better fenced in the North side of the
Church.
There are Twoe forms which stand in
the Chauncell equall with the
Communion Table on either side.
The leads over the Chauncell are much
decaied & if they be not speedily
repared it will quite ruinate the
Chauncell.
There is a place suncke in the
pavement of the Chauncell.

Lancing – St James the Less   *Storrington Deanery*

Incumbent	Patron (where known)
1602 – Walter Gibbons	Bishop of Lincoln
1610 – Walter Gibbons	
1636 – Timothy Holney	

1602   *(impropriator/farmer: William Peckham)*

The Chancell in defect in paving

The seates in the body of the Church at reparacions & the walles within wanteth bewtifying

3 November 1610

A water drippe in the belfrie

6 December 1636

There are twoe Seates which stand at each end of the Communion Table to be taken away. Their Church Bible is not of the last Translacion. They have noe Booke of Canons. Theire Booke of Common Praier is torne & not fitting. The Floore of the Church is unpaved in divers places. Many of the Seates in the body of the Church want plancking in the bottome. ~~The seeling of the Chauncell is gone to decay~~ & wantes reparing. The Church porch is unpaved & lyeth undecently. The Churchyard is much over growne with weeds & netles. The Fence of the South Side of the Churchyard is quite gone.
And the Churchyard lyeth altogeather open to another Cloase of land adioyning to the Southside thereof.
The Church is much annoyed and defiled with the dunging of Pigeons which Come into the Church and breed there.
The seeling of the Chauncell is much broken & decaied.
The Chauncell windowes are broken & pigeons come in thereat.
There are heapes of dust & rubbish in the Churchyard under the Church wall.
The Font will not hold water but they use a bason in the tyme of baptising.

Linchmere – St Peter   *Midhurst Deanery*

Incumbent	Patron (where known)
1602 – John Bennett	
1610	
1636 – Edward Cloweshay	

1602   *(impropriator/farmer: Thomas Cover)*

The sealing and pavinge in the Chauncell at defect

The communion table undecent
the seates not well flowered
one seate and the south dore at defect
the steeple wanteth [bordes]

30 October 1610

The lead of the steeple in decay, & the
healinge of the Church somewhat
decayed in the shingling

Littlehampton – St Mary   *Arundel Deanery*

Incumbent	Patron (where known)
1602 – William Parvise	
1610 – William Parvise	
1636 – Christopher Tuckey	Crown

1602

(impropriator/farmer: Henry Cook)

There wanteth seates
the walls need whitinge
the paving and glasse windows
mending

The seates to be repaired and plancked
the pavinge mendinge
the walls whitinge
the glas windowes and coveringe
repaired
the walles of the [south] side amended
they want a service booke and a decent pulpitt & a coveringe for the fonte

25 November 1636

The Chauncell wantes to be beautified with Sentences of Scripture.
The Chauncell wantes paveing.
The Windowes of the Chauncell want glaceing.
They want the Booke of homilies & a new Cloth & Cushion for the Pulpett & a Flaggon for the Communion wyne.
They have not the Service Booke for the 5th of November.
There is noe note indented of the utensills of the Church.
~~They have noe hood for the Minister~~.
There wantes a dore to the Minister's seate
The Bible wantes to be new Bound.
There wantes a new Cover for the Font & a new Beare; the old one is more like a ladder then Beere.
Many of the Seates in the Church want paveing or boarding in the bottoms.

Lodsworth – St Peter   *Midhurst Deanery*

Incumbent	Patron (where known)
1602 – Henry Lockett	Mountague family
1610 – Thomas Meeles	
1636 – Thomas Stevens	Crown

1602   *(impropriator/farmer: George Dennis)*

The Chauncell walles are faltie
the roofe is simmarly faltie
the glasse windowes want mendinge

The glasse windowes want mendinge
the seates are not planked nor paved underfoote
the Churche porche lackes a dore

11 November 1636

The ~~Church porch wantes to be all paved~~.

The Seates in the Chauncell stand equall with the Communion Table on Both sides.
They have not the Service Booke for the 5th of November.
They have noe Flaggon for the Communion wyne.
~~There are noe Sentences of Scripture sett up in the Chauncell~~.
There are Twoe Seates in the Chauncell which want plancking in the bottomes.
There wantes a more Convenient Seat for the Minister.

The Royal Coat of Arms of Charles I painted on the south wall of Burton church. Note the sentence of scripture written above the crest, intended to ensure that no-one was in any doubt where their allegiance should lie.

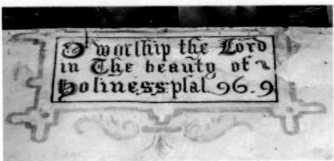

O worship the Lord in The beauty of Holiness psal 96.9

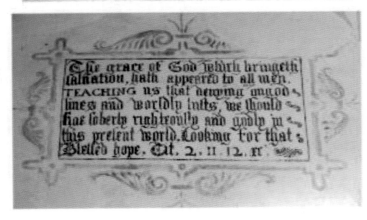

The grace of God which bringeth salvation, hath appeared to all men. TEACHING us that denying ungodliness and worldly lusts, we should lie soberly righteously and godly in this present world. Looking for that Blessed hope. Tit. 2. 11. 12. 13

Above: the interior of Burton church.

Above the fifteenth century screen the Decalogue can be seen, and on the walls are various sentences of scripture. The photographs on the previous page show these in detail.

It is still possible to make out small areas of colour on the screen, and on the extreme left of the photograph it is just possible to see part of the sixteenth century painting of St Uncumber above the Goring tomb.

Left:
The seventeenth century pulpit complete with tester in the church of St Botolph situated by the river Adur.

Right:
The seventeenth century pulpit with carved linenfold panels in St. Mary's West Chiltington.

Seventeenth century altar rails in St Peter and St Paul, West Wittering.

The church chest from St Mary Climping known as the Crusaders chest.

(our thanks to Rev Richard Hayes for permission to use this photograph in this volume)

Left:
Seventeenth century oak font cover in St James Heyshott.

Below:
Seventeenth century font cover in St Mary and St Gabriel South Harting.

Left:
An elaborate font cover from the Archdeaconry of Lewes in All Saints Mountfield. It was given to commemorate a wedding in 1581.

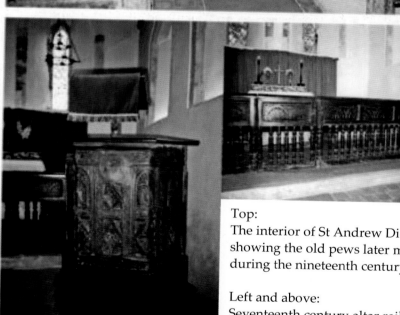

Top:
The interior of St Andrew Didling
showing the old pews later modified
during the nineteenth century.

Left and above:
Seventeenth century altar rail and
pulpit made from a seventeenth
century church chest.

Left:
The Communion Cup and lid used as a paten showing the date of 1568, from St Mary Aldingbourne.

Right:
The Communion Cup from St George Eastergate, also dated 1568 and thought to have been made locally.

(our thanks to Rev Martin Powell for permission for all these photographs to be used in this volume)

The Communion Cup and lid used
as a paten from St Peter Terwick,
dated 1569. Like the plate from
Aldingbourne and Eastergate, these
items are also thought to have been
made locally.

*(our thanks to Rev Edward Doyle for
permission for these photographs to be
used in this volume)*

Right:
The seventeenth century silver flagon for the communion wine from St Mary Billingshurst.

(our thanks to Rev David Beale for permission to use the photograph in this volume)

Left:
The seventeenth century pewter flagon for the communion wine from St John the Evangelist Bury.

(our thanks to Rev Peter Mallinson for permission to use the photograph in this volume)

In 1576 a fire destroyed the roof of St Mary and St Gabriel South Harting. The photograph shows the beautiful roof built to replace the one damaged in the Chancel.

Left:
The west tower of St Mary Stopham was rebuilt c.1600.

Below:
The west tower of St Mary Bepton showing the large seventeenth century brick buttresses needed to support the tower.

As change ringing of church bells became popular in the seventeenth century, and the shape of bells changed, stronger bell frames were required. The extra weight put a huge strain on the towers, which needed either rebuilding or strengthening.

Above:
An example of the type of bell frame needed to carry a number of bells. St Mary Rye in the Archdeaconry of Lewes.

Left:
A seventeenth century bell dated 1611 in St John the Evangelist Bury.

Above:
St Lawrence Lurgashall
has an unusual galleried
porch attached to the
south wall of the nave. Its
date is possibly sixteenth
century or even earlier.
The roof is made of
Horsham slab.

Left:
The brick south porch of
St Mary Stoughton was
built in the seventeenth
century.

It is still possible to see medieval wall paintings in a number of the churches.

Above shows the nave and into the chancel of St Botolph Hardham and right shows a detail depicting Adam and Eve from this church.

Below shows the nave of the little church at Coombes.

This small panel of stained glass is a portion of the original thirteenth century glass, and is set in the east window of North Stoke church.

The scene depicts the Coronation of the Blessed Virgin Mary, and it is thought that this is the earliest piece of glass with a figure subject in Sussex.

Lordington

Incumbent	Patron (where known)
1602 – Francis Heydon	Dean & Chapter
1610 – Francis Heydon	
1636 – Thomas Arderne	

1602

(impropriator/farmer: Francis Heydon)

The chappell ruinated & decayed
the roofe is uncovered [?]
the sealinge broke down
the walles unwhited & the windowe [?]

Lurgashall – St Lawrence   *Midhurst Deanery*

Incumbent	Patron (where known)
1602 – Ludovick Thomas	Viscount Mountague
1610 – Ludovick Thomas	
1636 – Thomas Stafford	William Yalden of Lodsworth

1602

The Chauncel wall in some places want roughcast
also the glase is faltie

The glase windowes are faltie
there wanteth pavinge in the Churche
the seates are ruinos not plancked nor paved

25 November 1636

The Chauncell wantes beautifying with
Sentences of Scripture.
There wantes a Cushion for the Pulpett
& a fairer Flaggon for the Communion
wyne.

Lyminster – St Mary Magdalene　　　　　*Arundel Deanery*

Incumbent	Patron (where known)
1602 – Anthony Hobson	Eton College
1610 – Thomas Hearne	
1636 – George Edgley	

1602　　　　　　　　*(impropriator/farmer: George Ansconn)*

The glas windowes and pavinge neede mendinge and the walles whitinge

The seates have neede to be repayred and plancked in the bottom
the walles whitinge
the pavinge to be mended
and the glas windowes at the west ende of the Churche doore at the same ende entringe into the Belfrye & the dore
one the South side of the Churche there is allso a chappell adioyninge unto the north side of the Chauncell very ruinos both in the timber worke of the roofe and covering
as allso walles pavinge & glasse windowes
there is allso one other chappel called St Stevens which is greatly decayed in the rooffe, walles, glasse windowes, and pavinge, and it ioyneth unto the north side of the Church

30 October 1610

The Church porch ill covered

25 November 1636

The Church wantes all to be new whited & adorned with Sentences of Scripture.
There is noe Table of the degrees of marriage.
There wantes a new Communion Booke; the old is torne in many places.

The Chauncell wantes paveing &
whiteing & to be beautifyed with
Sentences of Scripture.
There are some Seates in the Church
which want reparing.
They want twoe new Flaggons for the
Communion wyne.
The Challice is too litle.
There is noe Carpett for the
Communion Table nor cushion for the Pulpett.
There wantes a new Cover for the Font.
All the Fence of the Churchyard on the Northside of the Church is quite
ruynated & must be new made.

Madehurst – St Mary   *Arundel Deanery*

Incumbent	Patron (where known)
1602 – James Pellott	Thomas Page
1610 – James Pellott	
1636 – Toby Stubber	

1602
(impropriator/farmer: John Page)

The Chauncell glasse windows are in defalte

The Church is unpaved in many [parts?]
the seates are not sufficient
there is nether a pulpitt
the [minister's] seat is too lowe,
the glasse windowes are to be [?] glased

30 October 1610

The Church wanteth lighte the Church underneath kept, the groundsill of the porch defective & the steeple wanteth bording & pointinge, & a buttress at the Church somewhat in default

11 November 1636

There wantes a new Carpett for the Communion Table.
The Church ~~and Chauncell~~ want to be beautified with Sentences of Scripture.
There wantes a new Cloth & cushion for the Pulpett.
The Seates in the Church are very ruynous.

Merston – St Giles *Boxgrove Deanery*

Incumbent	Patron (where known)
1602 – Humphrey Booth	Crown
1610 – Humphrey Booth	
1636 – William Cox	

1602 *(impropriator/farmer: Humphrey Booth)*

The Chancell is unpaved in some parte
the glas windows want mendinge
the walles are unwhited

The Churche is decayed in the healinge and the north side
the glas windows are faltie
the north doore is undecent
the seates are faltie and the grounde in the seates is unseemely
the cover of the fonte is broken
the pulpit is unseemely

25 November 1636

There is noe Church Porch.
The Church wantes to be whited. And the Sentences of Scripture & the Kings
Armes which were sett up in the Church are almost worne out.
There is noe Cloth for the Pulpett.
There wantes a Cover for the Challice.
There is noe Booke of homilies nor Booke for the 5th of November.
The North side of the Chauncell wantes to be seperated from the Church.
There wantes a dore to the Chauncell & a Flaggon for the Communion wyne.
Divers of the seates in the Church are very ruinous.
The Beere whereon they carry the dead to Church is like a ladder.

Mid Lavant – St Nicholas

Boxgrove Deanery

Incumbent	Patron (where known)
1602 – William Devenish	Bishop of Chichester
1610 – Anthony Hopwood	
1636 – Robert Randall	

18 March 1603   *(impropriator/farmer: William Cobden)*

The Chauncell at the northside wanteth some tiling and within whitinge

The particion is all faltie betweene the Chauncell and Church where the bells hange and the southside of the Church wanteth some healinge

22 October 1610

The steeple unshingled some windows of the Church in parte stopped up

25 November 1636

All the South side and the East end of the Churchyard want to be fenced.
The Church porch wantes paveing.
The Church & Chauncell want to be all new whited and beautified with Sentences of Scripture.
There is noe Booke for the 5th of November, nor note indented of the Utensills in the Church.
There wantes a Canopy over the Pulpett and a Cover for the Font & a hood for the Minister.
Part of the windows in the Chauncell are dammed up to save charges of glaceing.
There are twoe great cracks in the Chauncell wall.
There is noe Table of the degrees of marriage.

Middleton – St Nicholas   *Arundel Deanery*

Incumbent	Patron (where known)
1602 – Jeremy Cooke	Crown
1610 – Jeremy Cooke/John Hughes	
1636 – Adam Page	

1602   *(impropriator/farmer: Jeremy Cook)*

The ground is uneven and unpaved
the walle cract and not well whited
the roofe wanteth to be better covered & the glas windowes to be amended

The steeple is very ruinos
the bodye [of] the Churche nether paved nor even
the roofe needeth mendinge
the walls neyther whited nor smothe
the seates homely
the glas windowes are in defalt
no particion betweene the Church and Chauncell
there is no porche

30 October 1610

The Church porch in default in healinge & the Church wall crackt & the
Church in decay in the shinglinge

6 December 1636

The Churchyard wantes to be fenced throughout.
The Chauncell wantes whiteing & to be beautified with Sentences of Scripture.
There is noe Ascent to the Communion Table.
The Communion Table is not railed in.
The Sentences of Scripture & the Kinges Armes are quite worne out.
The Chauncell wantes Covering in many places.
<u>There is no hood for the Minister.</u>

The Surplace is more like a shirt than a Surplace.
There is noe Booke of Cannons.
There is noe Flaggon for the Communion wyne.
There is noe Cloth nor lynnen for the Communion table.
Noe Booke for the 5th of November.
Noe Note indented of the Utensills of the Church.
Noe Beere to Carry the dead to Church but upon a ladder.
The Church wantes whiteing throughout.
The Church wantes paveing throughout.
No Cover for the Font.

Midhurst – St Mary Magdalene and St Denys   *Midhurst Deanery*

Incumbent	Patron (where known)
1602 – William Lacey	Mountague family
1610 – William Lacey	
1636 – William Fetherstone	

1602

The Chancell is unpaved in part
the seates unplancked
the glas windowes broken
a gutter between the Chauncell & my Lord's chappel at falte

The Churche is unpaved in a great part
the seates are unplancked
tenne seates decayed
the glas windowes full of holles
the tenn commandments nor lords prayer are not written ~~there~~
in the Roode loft the roofe at falte
~~ij seates~~
the Churche porch wants ij seates
the Churchyeard wanteth ij doors

30 October 1610

The Church ill healed on the north
and south & the porch also, the
communion table verie undecent &
the glass windowes much broken &
ruynous, and the Churchyard ill
fenced

25 November 1636

~~The flower of the Chauncell lyes very uneven & wantes paveing in divers places.~~

~~Ther are certain seates in the Chauncell which stand in both sides of the Communion Table & are equall height with it.~~

The Booke of homilies wantes to be new bound.

There wantes a new Communion Booke.

The Register Booke is to be made in better forme.

There wantes a new Cloth for the Pulpett and ~~another Flaggon for the Communion wyne~~.

The Ten Commaundments want to be new sett up in the Church.

The Church wantes whiteing throughout.

North Marden – St Mary

Incumbent	Patron (where known)
1602 – Richard Barwick	Bishop of Chichester
1610 – Henry Combe	Henry Shelley of Worminghurst
1636 – Thomas Hooke	Richard Brigham

1602 *(impropriator/farmer: Richard Barwick)*

The Chauncell unpaved & the seates to be repayred

The Churche unpaved & the seates
the porch unhealed & the sides want mending

22 October 1610

The Church verie darcke & wanteth light

North Mundham – St Stephen

Boxgrove Deanery

Incumbent	Patron (where known)
1602 – Daniel Hanson	Alexander & Joan Nowell of London
1610 – Daniel Hanson	
1636 – Joseph Lister	Thomas & Jane Bowyer

1602   *(impropriator/farmer: Mrs Boyer)*

The Chauncell pavement wanteth to be repaired
the east window hath iii or iiii quarrels to be amended

The Church wanteth pavement in divers places
the seates be much decayed
the flower underfoote neither borded nor paved
the Churche wolde require a window or two one the north and south side
the north doore wanteth locke and keye betweene the steeple and the Church
not close shutt together
the roofe is so open that it letteth the rayne into the Church
the porche flower is to lowe the water shooteth out of the Church yeard there
into

22 October 1610

The Church and porch
somewhat ill covered

1 December 1610

Our Chancell lyeth verie
ruinous wantinge much
reparacions both for tylinge
and glasinge

25 November 1636

Half the Churchyard towardes the north wantes to be railed or paled. And the Churchyard in generall wantes fencing.

~~There are dunghills made in the Churchyard~~.

The Church wantes healing in many places.

The Communion Table doth not stand North & South & is not railed in.

There are seats in the Chauncell which stand above the Communion table.

The Surplace is very ragged.

~~There is noe hood for the Minister~~.

There wantes a new Communion Book of the last edition.

The Church & Chauncell want to be new whited & adorned with Sentences of Scripture.

There is noe Table of the degrees of marriage, nor note indented of the utensills of the Church.

The Chauncell wantes reparing in the Covering in the outside.

There wantes a new Cover for the Font.

The Belfrey wantes paveing.

There wantes a better beere to carry the dead to Church.

There is no separacion between the Church & Chauncell.

The windowe at the lower end of the North side of the Church wants to be inlargeded & another window to be beaten out in the Southside of the Church; the same Church being very dark at the lower end therof.

North Stoke – St Mary the Virgin
Arundel Deanery

Incumbent	Patron (where known)
1602 – Thomas Heare	
1610 – Henry Spencer	
1636 – William Bray	Crown

1602

The seates of the Church underfoote are undecent
the timber worke in most of them is ruinos
the pavement glasse windowes and standing about the fonte are faultie
the walles in some places are to be whited
there is a drip or two in the roofe
the communion table is not decent
the lofte of the tower is decayed

30 October 1610

The south west end of the Church wall crackt, the south west corner of the Church ruynous

11 November 1636

The Church porch wantes paveing.
The South Isle & the North Isle in the Church want all to be paved.
There wantes a new Communion Table.
There wantes a better & larger seat for the Minister.
They have not the Booke for the 5th of November.
The Surplace is very badd & worne out.
There wantes a better Cloth & Cushion for the Pulpett & a better Carpett & lynnen Cloth for the Communion Table.
All the Seates in the Church want paveing or boarding in the bottomes.
The reading place is soe litle that the Minister can scarce stand in it.
There wantes a new Beere, the old one is like a ladder.
There is noe note indented of the utensills of the Church.
Many of the Seates in the Church are much fallen to decay.
There wantes a new Flaggon for the Communion wyne; the old one is altogeather unfitting.

Northchapel – St Michael
Midhurst Deanery

Incumbent	Patron (where known)
John Forman	

1602

The Chauncell walles lacke whitinge
the paving is faltie

Churchwardens [sic] are not plancked nor paved and have no doore
the steeple wanteth healinge
the steeple dore is ruinos without locke and keye

25 November 1636

The Church porch ~~is in~~ wantes great reparacions & it wantes paveing.
There are Seates which rancke themselves with the Communion Table.
The Chauncell wantes whiteing.
The Communion Table standeth not North & South.
The Chappell wantes paveing in every parte.
The Seates in the Chappell want much reparacions.
The Church wantes reparacions in the walls in divers places.
The Minister's seat is very dissightly & unfitting for him.
The Church wantes all to be new whited & the Sentences of Scripture to be sett up.
The place where the Communion Table standith being at the upper end of the Chauncell wantes to be all paved.
There is not a note indented in parchment of the utensills of the Church.
The Surplace is not soe sufficient as it should be.
They have noe Flaggon for the Communion wyne.

Nuthurst – St Andrew   *Storrington Deanery*

Incumbent	Patron (where known)
1602 – John Parcell	Crown
1610 – Jerome Beale	Bishop of Chichester
1636 – William Andrewes	

1602   *(impropriator/farmer: John Parcell)*

The Chauncell some part unpaved
the seates not planked

The steeple wantes shingling
the belfry in very mean estate for want of good postes and supporters
somewhat in defalte in the healing of the Churche

6 December 1636

~~The Register Booke is not made of parchment but of paper.~~
They wante a better Surplisse for the Minister, ~~a better Cloth & Carpett for the Communion Table.~~ These are all very old & not fitt to be used.
They have noe Chest to keepe the Register Booke and ornamentes, nor for the Almes for the poore.
There are some old decaied Seates in the Chauncell which ought to be amended or taken away.
The Table of the degrees of marriage is very old & almost quite consumed that it cannott be read.
The Roome adyoyning to the Church called the vestry is unpaved & lyeth very unseemly.
There is no Rope to ring the Saintes bell withall at the begynning of praiers.
The Church walles want whiteing, the Kinges Armes are defaced & ought to be new sett up.
The healing of the Church & Church porch want some reparing.
The Fence of the Churchyard is at default in many places.

Oving – St Andrew   *Boxgrove Deanery*

Incumbent	Patron (where known)
1602 – Ralph Widdowson	Henry Ball DD
1610 – Edward Martin	John Mattock DD
1636 – Thomas Carr	Thomas Lucas of Colchester

1602   *(impropriator/farmer: George Chatfield)*

The Chauncell wanteth repairing in the healinge
the glasse windowes want mendinge
the pavement is faltie
the walles unseemely
the south doore is badde

The Churche is decayed in the healinge
the walles are unseemely
the glas windowes are in decay
the pavements are not sufficient
the seates are divers of them unseemely
the grounde is not even
the font will hold no water
the particion betweene the Chauncell and the Church is not trimed
the Church doore one the north side is insufficient
the Church porche is faltie in the healinge
the seate for the minister to read prayers is not sufficient nether standeth conveniently
the steeple is faltie in the shingling and coveringe
one of the loftes under the bell is very badd

22 October 1610

The outleats of the Church in decay in the roofes, the porch ill covered

25 November 1636

There are divers dunghills lying in the Churchyard.

There are twoe posterne dores which open into the Churchyard.

The Westend of the Churchyard wantes to be all new fenced.

The Church porch wantes repacions in the Covering & to be all new paved.

The Chauncell wantes Covering in manie places alsoe it wantes to be whited and plaistered in th'inside.

There wantes a better Carpett for the Communion Table.

The Church wantes whiteing and to be adorned with Sentences of Scripture.

The Kings Armes are to be fairley sett up in the Church.

There wantes a new Table of the degrees of marriage.

There is noe note indented of the utensilles of the Church.

Parham – St Peter   *Storrington Deanery*

Incumbent	Patron (where known)
1602 – Robert Day	Crown
1610 – James Hutchenson	Sir Thomas Bishop
1636 – Richard Lewes	

1602   *(impropriator/farmer: Robert Day)*

The Chauncell is not paved at all but only an earthen flower with a badd matt upon it

The Church hath only a chalke flower
there are two seates downe
In Mr Busshoppes chappel the grounde is uncovered where Sir Thomas Palmer & his lady were buried

3 November 1610

The north est buttress faulty & there wants a pulpett to read prayers in

6 December 1636

There wantes a better Flaggon for the Communion wyne; That which they have is like an Alehouse Quart pott.
There are Seates which stand in equal rancke with the Communion Table.
~~There are Chestes standing by the Communion Table~~ which ought to be removed.
~~The Communion Table is not railed in.~~
~~The Communion Table is very old & unseemly & also too bigg for that litle Chauncell.~~
The walls of the Church want whiteing.
The Chest for Almes for the poore hath noe keyes & the lockes thereof are broken.
The other Chest for the Regyster booke hath but one ~~key~~ locke.
There is noe Booke of homilies nor Canons.

~~The seate wherein Sir Edward Bisshopps servauntes Doe sitt in the Chauncell is larger then needes & it standeth too neere to the Communion Table which ought to be taken away~~ & the seate to be made narrower.
The Ten Commaundmentes are soe defaced that they cannot be read; they ought to be sett up.
The Church & Chauncell are in decay in divers places.
The Church porch wantes paveing.

Petworth – St Mary   *Midhurst Deanery*

Incumbent	Patron (where known)
1602 – Alexander Bound	Eton College
1610 – Alexander Bound	
1636 – Richard Montagu	

1602

The walles want some poyntinge and roughe castinge in some places
the seates be unplancked in the bottome
the pulpitt wanteth a cover

30 October 1610

The windowe on the south side of the Church stopped up, & a window to be
mended on the north side the buttress on the north side of the Church porch in
defaulte & the porches ill healed

11 November 1636

The Chiefest part of the Pavement of
the Church is very much suncke
downe.
The Floore of the Church porch wantes
paveing.

Poling – St Nicholas   *Arundel Deanery*

Incumbent	Patron (where known)
1602 – John Ellis	Eton College
1610 – John Ellis	
1636 – Richard Mileson	

1602   *(impropriator/farmer: John Ellis)*

The Chauncell walles neede whitinge the pavinge glas windows and covering mending & the seates repairinge

They want a convenient seate for the minister to reade prayers in & a pulpitt
the communion booke the booke of homilies & Erasmus paraphrases need to be new bounde
the walles want whiting the seates repairing and plancking in the bottom
the glas windowes and covering want mendinge and also the pavinge wanteth mending
they want allso bell roopes and
the belfrie sealing needeth repairing

30 October 1610

To certify defects & repair

25 November 1636

The Churchyard wantes fencing in almost every part thereof.
They feed hoggs in the Churchyard usually.
There is a Barnes dore that opens into the Churchyard.
The Fermors gate on the Northside of the Church opens into the Churchyard.
~~The Churchwardens brought not the keyes of the Church for that it could not be viewed in the inside.~~

Pulborough – St Mary   *Storrington Deanery*

Incumbent	Patron (where known)
1602 – John Drury	John Apsley
1610 – John Drury	
1636 – Lawrence Pay	William Drury & George Apsley

[Nothing was provided on this church for any of the surveys. See Introduction for discussion]

Racton – St Peter   *Boxgrove Deanery*

Incumbent	Patron (where known)
1602 – Francis Heydon	
1610 – John Mead	Thomas Patterson, Archd Chichester
1636 – Thomas Aderne	Dean & Chapter

1602   *(impropriator/farmer: Francis Heydon)*

The seates in the Chauncell ruinos & no fit place for the minister to reade
divine service and the roofe wanteth healinge

The seates broken downe & very undecent
the pavement full of holles
the Churche porche unrepaired
the windowes not glased and the roofe dec[ayed]

25 November 1636

The Churchyard wantes all to be fenced throughout.
There wantes a new Communion Table and a cloth & carpett for the same.
The Communion Table is not railed in.
The Font hath no Cover.
The Chauncell wantes paveing in divers places also it wantes beautifying.
~~There be no hood for the Minister~~, nor the Booke for the 5th of November, nor
the Booke of homilies, nor the booke of homilies, nor Table of the degrees of
marriage, neither any note indented of the utensills of the Church.
They have noe Register Booke, they say they never had any.
They have not a Communion Booke.
The Bible wantes bindeing.
There is noe Beere to carry the dead to Church.

Rogate – St Bartholomew   *Midhurst Deanery*

Incumbent	Patron (where known)
1602 – Thomas Howsted	Crown
1610 – Thomas Howsted	
1636 – Thomas Littleton	

30 October 1610

The Church in decay in healinge on the north side

25 November 1636

There are dores which open into the Churchyard one in the occupacion of Ellis Hawes & th'other in th'occupacion of William Parkes

The Seates in the Chauncell rancke themselves with the Communion Table on both sides.

There are noe Sentences of Scripture sett up in the Chauncell.

The Chuch walls want plaistring in divers places and whiteing all over.

The Ten Commaundements & the Kings Armes which were sett up in the Church are quite worne out.

The Pulpett standeth within the Chauncell & hath noe Cover over it. And the Minister goeth up into the Pulpett upon a Ladder.

They have not the Service Booke for the 5th of November.

Theire Church Bible is not of the last Translacion.

They want the Booke of homilies.

They have noe note indented of the utensills of the Church.

They want another Flaggon for the Communion wyne; that which they have is not large enough.

There is noe hoode for the Minister.

The Chauncell wantes paveing.

The Pulpett Cushion is very badd & moth eaten.

They have noe Cloth for the Pulpett.

Rudgwick – Holy Trinity   *Storrington Deanery*

Incumbent	Patron (where known)
1602 – Nicholas Burrell	Bishop of Chichester
1610 – Nicholas Burrell	
1636 – Samuel Eborne	

1602   *(impropriator/farmer: William Faire)*

The Chauncell in defaltt in the shingles overheed
the doore into the Chauncell but weake and some three or more quarriels of glasse wantinge in the window

There wanteth some shingle in the steeple and a beame to be layde in the belfry
the ministers seat is not decent for want of bredth higthe and enclosure on the sides the depth is not well settled
the seates unplanked and some weake and tottering and a good parte of the Churche unpaved
the chapple annexed unto the Chauncell is unpaved

Rusper – St Mary Magdalene   *Storrington Deanery*

Incumbent	Patron (where known)
1602 – Joseph Browne	Cecilia Lewkenor
1610 – Joseph Browne	
1636 – William Pryaulx	John Mill

1602   *(impropriator/farmer: Joseph Browne)*

The Chancell within well only two buttresses [and] walles without are at reparacions

The Church is a little unpaved at the lower ende, the porch in decay

6 December 1636

They have not the Table of the degrees of marriage.

There are Seates in the Chauncell standing in equal height with the Communion Table.

There are some old Seates in the Chauncell which are much decayed & are very unseemly for the place.

~~The Font will not hold water to baptise children, but they use a painted earthen vessell in the Font.~~

~~The Stone worke about the Foot of the Font is loose & brooke & wantes reparing.~~

~~Theire Flaggon for the Communion wyne is not bigg enough; they want another.~~

~~The Fence of the Churchyard is at default in divers places.~~

Rustington – St Peter and St Paul   *Arundel Deanery*

Incumbent	Patron (where known)
1602 – Philip Somer	Bishop of Chichester
1610 – Philip Somer	
1636 – Silvester Adams	

1602   *(impropriator/farmer: Thomas Watersfield)*

The seates pavinge glasse windowes & coveringe neede repairinge

The seates neede both repairing and planckinge
the walls whitinge
the covering undecent especially over the south ile
the partition betweene the Churche and steeple repairing
there is no pulpitt and no surplice but a rage
there is also a chappel adionyinge to the Churche on the north side thereof
very ruinos both in the covering seelinge walls glasse windows & pavinge

30 October 1610

~~the south porch taken downe~~ a buttress of the Church faultie the communion
table undecent the north porch verie unborded & the west porch much
decayed

11 November 1636

There wantes a new Communion Booke & a new Communion Table, the old
being much decaied & very unseemly.
The Surplace is very old & badd.
~~They have noe Booke of homilies~~, nor Service Booke for the 5th of November.
Nor Table of the degrees of marriage.
There is noe note indented of the utensills of the Church.
There is a Dore which opens into the Chauncell & wantes reparing.
There are 4 or 5 dunghills in the Churchyard.
The North side of the Church wantes paveing.

Selham – St James   *Midhurst Deanery*

Incumbent	Patron (where known)
1602 – John Leigh	Thomas Bennett of Arundel
1610 – John Leigh	
1636 – John Pritchard	John Randall of Upwaltham

1602

[original entry for chw]
the seates are olde & not decent
the communion table wanteth mendinge

[entry at end of all the cases in a different hand, perhaps start of certificates?]
seates they are olde and not decente
for the reste of the steeple furniture within the Churche there is none
Communion Table it wanteth mendinge but they are about to mend it.
Be it knowne unto all men by these presente
That wee the Churchwardens of Sellham have taken a daye for the replacing
thereof and now it is fully repaired and amended

In witness whereof we heare presente
sett our handes
[this comes at the end of the surveys]

3 November 1610

The shingle on the north side of the
Church decaied the south ile of the
Church verie ruinous & supported
with wodden buttresses & the shingle
on the south side also faultie & the
porch likewise ii rafters of the Church
rotten the communion table & font
verie undecent

11 November 1636

~~The Church porch must be all new built by reason that the mayne foundacion is much suncke away & decaied.~~

The Church Bible is not of the last Translacion.

They have not the Service booke for the 5th of November.

The Communion Booke is not of the last edicion.

They want a new Communion Table.

The Chauncell walls want some plastring & whiteing.

The Sentences of the Scripture which are sett up in the Chauncell are almost worne out.

The ~~Ministers seat standeth in the Chauncell~~.

They have not a note indented of the utensills of the Church.

The Font is very foule in th'inside.

~~They have no Flaggon for the Communion wyne.~~

~~Theire Pulpett Cushion is too little & of too light a Colour.~~

There is no Clothe for the Pulpett.

Selsey – St Wilfrid   *Boxgrove Deanery*

Incumbent	Patron (where known)
1602 – Henry Harrison	Crown
1610 – Ludovick Bennett/	Bishop of Chichester
Francis Williams	
1636 – Anthony Farnedon	

18 March 1603   *(impropriator/farmer: Henry Harrison)*

The Chauncel wanteth much reparacions of square stones for the pavement
the walles discollored & in some [places] the plasteringe uncleered downe
the wainscott sealing over the communion table wanteth many bordes
the n[orth] side hath divers drippes
the seates and wanscott [d?] are ruinously decayed
the north window over growne with mosse
the dore into the Churchyarde is very much decayed and wolde be wanteth
locke and key

The Churche wanteth much pavinge
the ruinous seates at the west ende are divers of them cleane decayed
the south and north iles seates want to be erected
the ministers seate is 3 or 4 boords [fastened] together and a very homely deske
before this
[the] pulpitt wanteth steepes a doore and a deske
the [roofe?] hath many defaltes which cannot be mended but by scrippinge
thereof the north window is fowle and [dark]
the west & north doores are muche decayed [without] Loockes and hinges and
lockes and keyes.
The steeple hath many breches and stony windowes which lye open to all
[weather] muche decayeth it and the roofe wanteth healing
the steeple in many places wide open very hurtfull to the timber work and the

bells

the weather cock is blowne downe

25 November 1636

The Church porch wantes to be paved.

Both the outer Isles of the Church want to be new whited.

There wantes two new Flaggons for the Communion wyne, there being 300 communicants.

The Chauncell wantes whiteing & to be all new paved.

~~They have not the Booke for the 5th of November, nor the Booke of Canons~~ nor Table of the degrees of marriage, Nor note indented of the Utensills in the Church.

~~There is noe hood for the Minister.~~

The Chauncell wantes repairing in the Covering thereof.

The Bible is not of the last Translacion.

The Font will not hold water & hath not a fitting Cover.

Shipley – St Mary   *Storrington Deanery*

Incumbent	Patron (where known)
1602 – Thomas Pritchard	
1610 – Thomas Pritchard	
1636 – Edward Tredcroft	

1602   *(impropriator/farmer: John Henley)*

The Chauncell not thoroughly paved
the seates are not plancked

Some few stones are slyde from the healinge and here and there a shingle from
the steeple

6 December 1636

The Communion Table is very old & unseemly; they want a new one.
The Carpett for the Communion Table is old & worne out; there wantes a new.
The ~~Communion Table is not placed at the upper end of the Chauncell nor railed in~~.
~~They have not the Booke of homilies nor hood for the Minister.~~
~~The healing of the Chauncell is much at default & a great part therreof is quite fallen down.~~
~~The walls of the Chauncel want whiteing in the inside.~~
The Ten Commaundmentes want to be sett up more plainly.
The Church walls want mending & whiteing on the inside.
Many ~~of the seates in the body of the Church are much broken & decayed & want reparing.~~
~~The Fence of the Churchyard is very much in decay so that hoggs may easily come in at divers places.~~
The Steeple wantes shingling very much.
There is a house adjoining to the Churchyard which hath twoe dores opening
onto the Churchyard And there is a garden plott laid to the same house which
is wholly taken out of the ground of the Churchyard.

Sidlesham – St Mary

Boxgrove Deanery

Incumbent	Patron (where known)
1602 – William Whalley	Prebendary of Sidlesham
1610 – William Whalley	
1636 – John Taylor	

1602 *(impropriator/farmer: George Green)*

The Chauncell wanteth some fewe square stones to amende the pavement
the roofe wanteth reparacion
the glas windowes are at defalte

Both the iles and seates hath there [?] much broken
the seates in those iles are exceedingly in decaye
the roofe of the Church hath divers dripps
the pulpitt wanteth steepes & a doore and a sound borde over the heade
the belfry flower is much bro[ken]
the steeple windowes lie open and is hurtfull to the timber workes
the wheels of the bells are decayed
the porch wanteth eche side bordes for the backe and there is a drippe in the roofe thereof

22 October 1610

The Church windowes in parte stopped up with stones the south outlett in decay in the timber worke of the roofe the shingles of the steeple somewhat in decay and the porch likewise, the ministers seate and communion table undecent

[November] 1636

To repar the Fence of the Churchyard
to prevent the posterne dores going into the Churchyard and whose they are
to make a partition betweene the Church and Chauncell; to newe white the Church

to present those that hath seates in the Church or Chauncell which seemilie kept to [meld] the Communion table;
to provide A new carpet for the Communion table and A bible of the last translation;
to provide A note of the utenseles of the Church
To repare the dec[ay] of the belfrie;

to provide A new flagon for the Communion table and A better linnen Clothe for the Communion table;
to present the decaie of the Chauncell and to see the seats pull downe, the Seats Chaun[cell] which stands equall with the Communion table.

Singleton – The Blessed Virgin Mary   *Boxgrove Deanery*

Incumbent	Patron (where known)
1602 – John Chauntler	Sir John Lumley
1610 – John Chauntler	
1636 – John Chauntler	

1602   *(impropriator/farmer: John Allen & Wm Love)*

The pavinge seates and windowes of the Chauncell want mendinge
the Chauncell wanteth some hea[ling]

The Churche wanteth pavinge, and the windowes glasinge
the ministers seate is undecent
the southe dore at falte
the steeple at muche falte in the roofe
the porche unpaved and the stayers of the chamber over the porch like to fall
down the ridging on the south side of the Church wanteth mendinge

22 October 1610

The porch and steeple decaied in reparacions and a whole window in the
Church stopped up the communion table undecent, & a buttresse of the
Church porch like to fall downe

[November] 1636

The Parsons Fence against the
Churchyard wantes paling or railing.
The Church porch wantes paveing.
The seats in the Chauncell want
paving.
There is no Canopy over the Pulpett.
There wantes a new Carpett for the
Communion Table.

The Chauncell wantes plaistering.

There is no Chest to keep the Register Booke in, nor a book for 5th November.

Theire Booke of Cannons, Booke of homilies nor Bishop Jewelles works are not kept in the Church.

~~There wantes a reading place for the Minister~~.

There is no note indented of the utensilles of the Church, nor hoode for the Minister.

The Font wantes a new Cover.

The Church wantes whiteing & plaistering in many places.

The south Isle of the Church wantes paveing.

The Ten Comaundments & the Kings arms want to be new sett up in the Church.

Slinfold – St Peter

Storrington Deanery

Incumbent	Patron (where known)
1602 – Philip Mustian	Bishop of Chichester
1610 – Philip Mustian	
1636 – John Scull	

1602 *(impropriator/farmer: Philip Mustian)*

The Chauncell wanteth paving

It is needfull that the Churche in the healinge overhead shoulde be all poynted for the preservinge of the roofe
the wall withinside to be whited
the windowes want glasing
the belfry wantes bordinge
the Church porch wanteth healinge
an arche in the wall one the southside of the Church to be mended
defalte in a gutter for the want of leade in a chappel & some glasse wantinge in a windowe of the same chappell

30 October 1610

The steeple in decay in healinge there wanteth a payr of stayers & the steeple verie weake & shaketh much the east buttress much decayed & the Church verie ill healed

6 December 1636

~~The Communion Table is not railed in.~~
~~There are seates & formes which stand by the Communion Table & in equall height with it.~~
There want dores {double dores} betweene the Church & Chauncell.
The Pavement of the Church is broken & at default in divers places.
The Church porch wantes some boarding.

Divers pannells of the Fence of the Church porch are in sufficient & ought to be new made answerable to the rest.

~~The Ten Commaundmentes are soe obscured & defaced that they can hardly be read.~~

~~The healing of the Church is at default in divers places.~~

~~The Church wantes to be new whited in the inside, or at least the dust & soile to be rubbed of the walls.~~

There is a house adioyning to the Churchyard which has a topp windowe & a Back dore opening into the same. The inhabitants in that howse have made a sincke or Gutter out in the Churchyard into the which they poore out theire fowle water. And also they empty theire Chamber pottes out of the upper windowe into the Churchyard.

~~They have not the Booke of Canons~~ nor the Booke of homilies.

They have not a chest for Almes for the poore, but onely the chest wherein the Register Booke and the ornamentes are kept.

Sompting – St Mary
Storrington Deanery

Incumbent	Patron (where known)
1602 – John Gibson	Sir John Caryll
1610 – John Gibson	
1636 – William Linnett	

1602   *(impropriator/farmer: Richard Grave)*

The Chauncel is in defect in pavinge & the windows in glasinge

A chappel at the northside of the Church is at defalte in timberinge and some layinge of stones
the seates in some places want mendinge and the Churche within whitinge and bewtifyinge and the windows in defalte of glasinge

3 November 1610

The seelinge of the Church faultie

6 December 1636

The Seates on both sides stand equall with the Communion Table. The Church porch is unpaved & the Floor lyes uneven & undecent.
There wantes a better Booke of Common Praier & the largest volume.
They want the Booke of Canons & the Booke of homilies.
They have noe Flaggon for the Communion wyne.

South Harting – St Mary and St Gabriel   *Midhurst Deanery*

Incumbent	Patron (where known)
1602 – John Shorter	Elizabeth Beligram
1610 – John Shorter	Elizabeth Beligram
1636 – John Lesley	Crown

1602   *(impropriator/farmer: John Shorter)*

The Chauncell wanteth a doore upon the northside which lyeth open to the vestrie
three windows on the northside are unglased
one windowe on the east side unglased
the glasse is broken in two windowes one the south side and in one windowe on the north
the Chancell wolde be wasshed
the south dore wants a keye and one henge

The Church wantes healinge it rayneth in divers places
the seats are unplancked
the windows want xxvi quarrells of glasse at the least
the south dore must be renewed
the minister wants a seate to read divine prayer he is forced to read prayer standinge
the Church wants whitinge
the south doore wolde be renewed for it is decayed
the south ile is unpaved
the walles neede morteringe
the wall of the east side of the Churchyard is decayed

25 November 1636

The surplice is torne & Quite worne out.

There is no hoode for the Minister.

The walls of the Chauncell want whiteing & there are noe Sentences of Scripture sett up there.

The Ten Commaundments & the Kings Armes which were sett up in the Church are quite worne out.

They have not the Booke of homilies nor the Booke of Canons.

They want another Flaggon for the Communion wyne.

They have not the Service Booke for the 5th of November nor a note indented of the utensills of the Church.

The Church porch wantes paveing.

There is no Cover for the Pulpett.

There wantes a new Communion Booke & a Cloth & Cushion for the Pulpett.

The Chauncell wantes plaistring & reparing in manyplaces.

The Pavement of the Church is very uneven & many of the seates want plancking in the bottomes.

The Church wantes whiteing throughout.

There wantes a Cover for the Font.

All the Sentences of Scripture which are sett up in the Church are quite worne out & scarce perceivable.

South Stoke – St Leonard   *Arundel Deanery*

Incumbent	Patron (where known)
1602 – John Browning	Earl of Arundel
1610 – John Browning	
1636 – Simon Bankes	

1602

The rofe of the Churche hath in it some few drippes
the seates are to be amended some faltes are in the walles

11 November 1636

Both Church & Chauncell want whiteing & Beautifying with Sentences of
Scripture.
~~The Communion Table doth not stand North & South, neither is it sett Cloase
to the wall at the upper end of the Chauncell~~.
The Raile which is sett before it is very meane & not fitting.
There wantes a better Carpett for the Communion Table, the old is very poore
& meane.
The Cloth & Cushion for the ~~Pulpett for the~~ Pulpett are very old & moth eaten.
All the Seates in the Church in generall all want much reparing & also
boarding or paveing in the bottoms.
There wantes a new Beere, the old is like a ladder.
There wantes a new Surplace, the old being very old & too short.
There is no Booke of homilies or the booke for the 5th of November
There is noe note indented of the utensills of the Church.
The Churchyard wantes fenceing in many places.

Stedham – St James   *Midhurst Deanery*

Incumbent	Patron (where known)
1602 – John Taylor	
1610 – John Taylor	
1636 – Joseph Henshaw	Crown

1602   *(impropriator/farmer: Anthony Aylwin)*

The Chauncell wanteth healinge walles & glas windowes
at some defect in pavinge
the seates one the northside badly flowered

The Churche roofe wanteth closinge to the steeple
wantes the walles untrimmed
the pavinge somewhat broken
the seates for the most parte badd & ill flowered
the communion table not sufficient and the porche at reparacions

25 November 1636

The Church walls want whiteing.
The Chauncell wantes whiteing.
They have not Service Booke for the 5th of November, nor the Booke of
Canons, nor the Booke of homilies.
~~They have noe hood for the Minister.~~
They have noe note indented of the utensills of the Church.
There wantes a new Pulpett and a new Seate for the Minister to reade divine
service in.
The Church porch wantes to be decently paved.
The Sentences of Scripture which are sett up about the Chauncell are quite
worne out.
The Register Booke wantes to be new bound.
They want a new Communion Booke and another Flaggon for the Communion
wyne.

Steyning – St Andrew   *Storrington Deanery*

Incumbent	Patron (where known)
1602 – Stephen Vinall	Sir John Shirley
1610 – Jonas Michael	Sir John Shirley
1636 – Leonard Stallman	Lord George Goring

1602

The Chauncel within is very ruinous and hath not bin occupied of longe time by reason the windows are unglazed the walles unpoynted and unwhited the roofe is unsealed & the flower unpaved lying very undecent So that it is now a common haunt for pigions

The roofe of the Churche in the healinge is faultie in sundrie places whereby it often rayneth down in to the Churche

the walles are not well whited and bewtified within but in some places are unpainted.

The hiest windows on the north side of the Churche are unglazed and in divers other windowes the glasse here or there broken

the seates are the most parte of them very ruinous & badd

the flower is in sundrie places unpaved.

The pulpit olde and badd

the fonte wanteth a decent cover and the south dore is not good

3 November 1610

The Church on the south side faultie in healinge, the porch faultie in healinge likewise two buttresses of Church porch faultie & in decay, the bottom of the buttress on the north west in decay also

6 December 1636

They want a new Common Praier Booke.

~~They have noe hoode for the Minister.~~

The pavement of the Chauncell wantes mending in some places.

Sir Edward Bellingham's Chauncell wantes reparing in the seating, And alsoe it wantes paveing. Sir John Leedes his Chauncell wants paveing.

They want twoe bigger Flaggons for the Communion wyne.

Theire Booke of homilies is very old & torne; they want a new one.

Divers seates in the Church want reparing both in the sides & bottomes.

Stopham – St Mary   *Midhurst Deanery*

Incumbent	Patron (where known)
1602 – Thomas Charman	William Bartlett
1610 – Laurence Pay	Bishop of Chichester
1636 – William Chandler	Crown

4 November 1610

The north west corner of the Church wall crackt
the south west buttress of the steple faulty,
the rafters on the south side of the Church faulty and rotten and there wanteth
a preaching pulpett

11 November 1636

The Churchyard wanteth to be
fenced in many places.
There is a Grave suncke in the
Chauncell which lyeth very
unseemely.
The Church & Chauncell are to be
beautified with Sentences of
Scripture.
They want the service Booke for the
5th of November.
They have not a note indented of the utensills & ornaments of the Church.
The lower Belfrey is very much gone to decay & wantes boarding & the mayne
timber of the Steeple is fallen much to repacions.
They have noe Chest for Almes for the Poore.
The Communion Table is very badd & rotten.

Storrington – St Mary   *Storrington Deanery*

Incumbent	Patron (where known)
1602 – Edward Wickham	Crown
1610 – Edward Wickham	
1636 – William Mattock	Anthony Mattock & Gregory Duckett

1602

The Chauncel wanteth pavinge & the walles whitening

The Churche wanteth a comly pulpitt
the windows are much broken
the body of the Churche is unpaved in many places
the Chauncel which appertayneth unto the parishe is almost wholy unpaved & it wanteth a payer of dores
the walles lacke whitinge & the seates being not bottomed with bordes lye like graves

3 November 1610

The buttress on west end of the Church faultie the south west corner of the Church verie ruynous the cover of the font & communion table very undecent, a gutter between the parson's Chancell & the parishioners at defaulte

6 December 1636

There wantes a bigger Flaggon for the Communion wyne.
The Register Booke is not kept in the Chest in the Church But in the Parsons house.

Stoughton – St Mary

Boxgrove Deanery

Incumbent	Patron (where known)
1602 – Nicholas Diggins	Crown
1610 – Matthew Major	Bishop of Chichester
1636 – Matthew Major	

1602   *(impropriator/farmer: George Gunter)*

The seates in the Chauncell pavement and glasse of the windows decayed

~~The Church and~~ pavement in the alleys broken upp
the seates unborded
the belfry not plancked
the walles want whitinge and the outside reparinge and the church porche
reddie to fall downe

[November] 1636

The Church & Chauncell are over growne with Ivy.
The Church porch wantes to be paved.
There wantes a Canopy for the Pulpett.
The Seates in the Chauncell want to be either paved or plancked & the
Chauncell wantes to be ~~either~~ levelled or paved.
The Steeple is cracked for the topp to the bottome on the South side.
The Seates in the Chauncell are very much decaied & ruynated.
There wantes a new Cover for the Font, Alsoe the Font wantes whitening.
There is noe Book of Homilies nor Booke for 5th of November nor note
indented of the utensills of the Church nor Table of the degrees of marriage.
There is noe Flaggon for the Communion Wyne, here being about 200
Communicantes.
The dorr in the Chauncell is very much decaied & broken.
There wantes a more decent raile for the Communion Table.
The West dore of the Church is very much decaied & rotten.
The glasse windowes in the Chauncell are broken in many places.
The Challice is broken & is as thin as paper.

Sullington – St Mary   *Storrington Deanery*

Incumbent	Patron (where known)
1602 – William Wady	Thomas Bennett
1610 – John Leeme	
1636 – Hugh Robinson	Peter Cox & John May

1602   *(impropriator/farmer: William Wady)*

The Chauncel wanteth pavinge and the walls whitinge

The main wall of the Church is rent from the tope to the bottom on the north side & the rooffe beames are all slydden out of the wall
the walls within want whiting there wanteth some pavinge in the body of the Churche
the great and used dore one the south side is [naughty] and the locke badd
the walles of the steeple are overgrown with ivie which hurteth them
there is a butresse on the south side falinge downe
there is one seate in the Church downe which must be redified by John Haines and divers other seates want plankinge
there wanteth pavinge in the steeple goinge out at doore

6 December 1636

~~The Communion Table is not railed.~~
~~The Chauncell walls want white lymeing & whiteing in the Inside.~~
The Seates in the Chauncell want boarding or paving in the bottomes.
The Chauncell windows are much broken.
There wants a better & larger Carpett for the Communion Table.
There wantes a bigger Flaggon for the Communion wyne.
They want a Booke of Canons & the Booke of homilies.

They have noe Chest for Almes for the poore but only the chest wherein the Register booke & ornamentes are to be kept.

~~Divers of the Seates in the Church are in decay.~~

~~The Font wantes paveing, it is in decay; they use to sett a bason of water in it where there is any child to be baptysed.~~

The Church wants some paynting in the healing therof.

The Flower of the Church porch is unpaved & lyeth uneven & very undecent.

The Church bible is not of the last Translacion.

The Church walls are very much over growne with Ivy which is very hurtfull to the same walles.

Sutton – St John   *Midhurst Deanery*

Incumbent	Patron (where known)
1602 – Ludovic Lewes	Archbishop of Canterbury
1610 – Ludovic Lewes	Earl of Northumberland
1636 – Aquila Cruso	

1602   *(impropriator/farmer: Ludovic Lewes)*

The Chauncell lacketh some glasinge and a [little] mendinge of the wall
without and the stee[ple]

The belfrye is not whited
there is a littell partition of the northside lacketh pavinge
certayne holes to be plastered and a comly communion table and a better
pulpitt

30 October 1610

The communion table undecent there wanteth a preaching pulpett the west
dore verie badd the Church in decay in covering on the north side

25 November 1636

The Churchyard wantes fencing everywhere.
The Churchyard wall wantes reparing.
~~The Churchyard is to be clensed throughout~~.
The Church porch is to be new built.
The Ten Commaundments and other Sentences of Scripture are to be fairly sett
at the East end of the Church.
They want a Chest for Almes for the poore.
The Register booke wantes to be new bound.
They have not a note indented of the utensills which belonge to the Church.
The Communion Table is to be set cloase to the East wall of the Chauncell &
the devision is to be pulled downe. ~~And the lower ground of the Chauncell to
be made even with the lower upper ground thereof.~~

Terwick – St Peter

Midhurst Deanery

Incumbent	Patron (where known)
1602 – John Shorter	Peter Betsworth of Rogate
1610 – John Shorter	
1636 – Peter Draper	

1602

the seate for the [minister] is not sufficient

30 October 1610

To certify defects and repair

25 November 1636

The Church porch wantes much reparing in the Covering.

The Church walls want whiteing & Sentences of Scripture to be sett up.

The Church is not beautified at all.

The Ten Commaundments are not fairly set up.

The Kings Armes are to be sett up.

The walles of the Chauncell want whiteing.

The Communion Table is not railed in.

There wantes a new Communion Table & a Cloth for the pulpett & a Surplce for the Minister.

They want the Table of the degrees of marriage & a new Booke of homilies.

They have noe Flaggon for the Communion wyne.

They want the Service Booke for the 5th of November.

They have noe note indented of the utensills of the Church.

They have not the Booke of Cannons.

The Fence of the Churchyard neere the gate wantes reparing.

They have no Chest for Alms for the Poore.

Thakeham – St Mary   *Storrington Deanery*

Incumbent	Patron (where known)
1602 – Michael Ward	
1610 – John Tichbourne	Robert Tichbourne of London
1636 – Thomas Banks	Edward Apsley

1602

The Chauncell windowes wante some glasinge & the flower unpaved

In the Church there wanteth a comvenient seate for the minister to saye service
in all the womens seates are rotten and nought and must be new made
the windowes lacke some glasinge
the walls want whiting
the seates are not borded in there bottomes

Tillington – All Hallows

Midhurst Deanery

Incumbent	Patron (where known)
1602 – Lawrence Alcock	Thomas Stanley
1610 – Lawrence Alcock	
1636 – Thomas Alcock	

1602

The walles are not whited nor paynted

the pavinge is faltie in some place

the seates are olde and unplancked in the bottom, without dores,

the pulpitt is not sufficient it standes to lowe without a cover and wanteth a doore

11 November 1636

The Byble is not of the last Translation.

They have not the Service Booke for the 5th of November.

The Chauncell walls want beautifying.

They have not a note in parchment indented of the utensills of the Church.

There wantes a new Booke of Common praier.

Tortington – St Mary Magdalene   *Arundel Deanery*

Incumbent	Patron (where known)
1602 – William Grundell	John Browne
1610 – Oliver Brunsell	Sir William Gratwick
1636 – Adam Page	Crown

1602

There is but one place to read prayers
and to preach which is to be made
larger and the waye into it to be
altered,
the seates to be mended
some places to be paved
the Church is very darke by reason the
windowes are closed up which wold
be glased
the roofe to be new poynted

25 November 1636

The Churchyard wantes fenceing every where.

The Church wantes to be all new whited & beautifyed with Sentences of the Scripture and with the Kinges Arms.

The Chauncell wantes to be whited & beautifyed with Sentences of Scripture.

There are some Seates in the Chauncell which rancke themselves with the Communion Table.

~~There is noe hood for the Minister; he being~~ a Master of Arts.

There wantes a new Surplice, a new Cloth for the Pulpett & a Booke of homilies & a Service Booke for the 5th of November.

There is noe note indented of the utensills of the Church.

Theire Bible is not of the last Translacion.

There is noe Flaggon for the Communion wyne.

There wantes a new Communion Booke & the old is much torne & is not of the last edicion.

Treyford – St Mary

Midhurst Deanery

Incumbent	Patron (where known)
1602 – Thomas Wall	John Tregost
1610 – Thomas Wall	
1636 – John Hayes	William Alwyn

1602   *(impropriator/farmer: Thomas Wall)*

The Chauncell is uncovered one the southside & northside
the windowes want glasing
the shingles are clean worne oute
there is but one seate in the Chancell and it is very ruinous & unplancked
the flower is greate parte of it unpaved and lyeth most filthily
~~the communion table is nest betweene the belfrie by reason of [water?]~~

The walls want mortering and wasshing
the walles on the outside be ruinous and will fall excepte they be with all
speede amended
the oves about the Chauncell be open

The oves be open
the inside of the wall that ioyneth to the roofe is ruinous and wanteth
mortering & wasshing
the seates unplancked
the Church porch uncovered in the roofe and the estside the outside of the wall
full of holes and in short time will decay
the particion betweene the Chauncell and the Church very unseemely
there is but one bell which hangeth in the Chauncell & no steeple
the foote of the fonte wold be repaired
one window unglased the rest broken & full of holles

25 November 1636

The Church Porch and the Seates therein want reparcions.
All the Church wantes whiteing.

The Chauncell wantes whiteing all about and there are not any Sentences of Scripture sett up about it.

The Ten Commaundments also other Sentences of Scripture & the Kings Armes which are sett up about the Church are almost worne out.

There is no Cover over the Pulpett.

They have not the Booke of homilies, nor the Booke of Canons, nor the Service booke for the 5th of November.

They have not a note indented of the Utensills of the Church.

There is noe hoode for the Minister nor Cloth for the Pulpett.

Part of the Fence on the North side of the Churchyard is gone to decay and wantes to be new made.

Trotton – St George   *Midhurst Deanery*

Incumbent	Patron (where known)
1602 – Francis Purslowe	Crown
1610 – Robert Tomlinson	
1636 – Robert Tomlinson	

1602   *(impropriator/farmer: Francis Purslowe)*

The Chauncell windowes want glasinge the seates mending and the Chauncell pavinge

The healinge walles glasinge paving and south doore at reparacions
the pulpit and moste of the seates insufficient
the residew badly flowred
the flower of the steeple wanteth bordes

25 November 1636

The Chauncell wantes some whiteing.
The Church wantes to be new whited.
They have noe note indented of the utensills of the Church.
The Ten Commaundements & other Sentences of Scripture about the Church want to be new sett up.
The Covering of the Chauncell wantes some reparacions.

Tuxlith – (no known dedication)   *Midhurst Deanery*

Incumbent	Patron (where known)

1602   *(impropriator/farmer: Francis Purslow)*

The Chauncel two windowes unglassed not paved

The Church in defecte in healing
an insufficient seate for the minister
the desk is but mean for the bible
i window unglased there wanteth par[..?]

Upmarden – St Michael   *Boxgrove Deanery*

Incumbent	Patron (where known)
Upmarden with Compton	
1602 – Richard Barwick	Lord Montague and Roger Bringborne
1610 – Richard Barwick	Lord Montague and Roger Bringborne
1636 – Anthony Gray MA	Thomas Gray of Woolbeding

1602   *(impropriator/farmer: Richard Barwick)*

The Chancel is unpaved

There is no pulpitt but the seate for service in the Church

22 October 1610

There wanteth a pulpett
the Church hath a drip in the north east side,
the font uncovered
there wanteth a communion table

[November] 1636

The Churchyard must be fenced throughout.
The Church wantes paving in many places.
The Chauncell lyith after a very vast manner, & it wantes paveing and levelling throughout & all to be paved.
The Communion table standeth not within the Raile.
There is no hood for the Minister.
The Surplace is old & rotten.
The Seats in the Chancell are very ruynous.
They have not the book for the 5th of November.
The Reading place wantes to be raised higher.
There wantes a new Cover for the Font & it wantes to be whited.
There is no particion betweene the Church and Chauncell.

There wantes another Flaggon for the Communion wyne.

There is noe Table of the degrees of marriage, nor note indented of the utensils of the Church.

The Belfrey wantes paveing.

There is no Chest for Almes for the poore.

The Chest wherein the Register book is kept standeth within the Rayle.

The Church generally wantes reparing.

There is noe Beare to carry the dead to Church.

Upwaltham – St Mary

Incumbent	Patron (where known)
1602 – John Lee	Dorothy Dawtrey
1610 – John Lee	
1636 – David German	Mary Dawtrey of Petworth

1602   *(impropriator/farmer: John Lee)*

The Chauncell is decayed in the healinge
the glasse is faltie
the walles are not whited & have some holes in them

The Church is faltie in the healinge
the walles are unseemely
the windowes brocken
the Church porche is faltie in the healinge and growne pinninge

25 November 1636

The Churchyard lyeth very ruinous. And it wantes fencing throughout. Also
~~there are divers dunghills in the Churchyard~~.
The Church Porch wantes silling & to be all paved.
The Church wantes all to be new whited & beautified with Sentences of
Scripture.
~~The Church wantes paveing in many places.~~
There wantes a new Pulpett & reading place for the Minister.
~~The Glasse windowes in the Chauncell are very much broken.~~
~~There wantes a new Communion Table & a raile about it.~~
There wantes a new Carpett for the Communion Table.
There is noe Chest for Almes for the poore, nor for the Register Book.
~~There are Twoe Seates in the Chauncell which want plancking or paveing.~~
~~There is noe Pulpett Cloth nor Cushion, nor Flaggon for the Communion~~
~~wyne.~~

Walberton – St Mary   *Arundel Deanery*

Incumbent	Patron (where known)
1602 – Edmund Meadowcroft	Bishop of Chichester
1610 – Edmund Meadowcroft	
1636 – Thomas James	

1602   *(impropriator/farmer: Richard Mothe)*

The Chauncel is unpaved but the grondde is even
the glasse windows are in some defalte

There wanteth a pulpitt and [pew] to reade prayers in the old are not decent
there are many places unpaved
the Churche is very darke

3 November 1610

A buttress on the south est faulty, the porch in decay the Church wants light

25 November 1636

The Church wantes to be all new whited & beautified with the Kinges Armes &
with Sentences of Scripture.
The Chauncell wantes whiteing & to be beautified with sentences of Scripture.
Theire Church Bible is rent & torne in many places.
There is noe Booke of homilies nor note indented of the Utensills of the
Church.
There wantes a more Convenient Seat for the Minister for it standith in the
Chauncell soe that the greatest part of the Congregacion cannott heare the
Minister.
The wyndowes in the Chauncell want glaceing.
There wantes a new Carpett for the Communion Table & a new Cushion for
the Pulpett.
Theire Flaggon for the Communion wyne is like an Alehowse pott.
There is noe Chest for Almes for the Poore.

Warminghurst – The Holy Sepulchre   *Storrington Deanery*

Incumbent	Patron (where known)
1602 – William Pratt	Henry Shelley
1610 – William Pratt	
1636 – Stephen Goffe	Edward Apsley

1602

The Chauncell flower lacketh a litle pavinge and the walls whitinge

In the Church some parte of the roolfe is uncovered
the walles lacke whitinge
the seates are without bottomes of bordes

3 November 1610

The communion table undecent & the porch faultie in healinge

6 December 1636

~~There Font will not hold water so that they are forced to use a bason which they put therein to hold the water for Baptisme.~~
They have not the Booke of Canons nor the booke of homilies.
There booke of Common Praier is old & torne & not of the last edition, viz. it is 30 yeares old.

Warnham – St Margaret   *Storrington Deanery*

Incumbent	Patron (where known)
1602 – Matthew Allen	Dean & Chapter of Canterbury
1610 – Michael Birkhead	
1636 – Thomas Holland	

1602

There wanteth some pavinge in the Churche where burial hathe bin & some pavinge in the chappel

some iij or iiij stones sliped from the coveringe of the Churche.

The seates most of them unplanked

30 October 1610

The Church and porch wants pointinge

6 December 1636

~~The Fence of the Churchyard is much at default in most places.~~

There is an outhowse adioyning to the Church heretofore use for a belfry or some such use which is greatly fallen to decay.

~~There is a dunge heape or dust heape lying behinde the Church porch against the Churchwall.~~

~~There are divers holes in the healing of [?] Michell's Chauncell & the pavement of the same is faulty~~ & broken in many places.

The Communion Table is not sett at the upper end of the Chauncell & is not railed in.

There are divers Seates standing about the Communion Table & some above it.

Divers of the Seates in the Church want boarding in the bottoms & allso want other reparacions.

The Church Bible is not of the last Translacion being printed Anno 1583.

They have not the Table of the degrees of marriage.

Warningcamp – (no known dedication)   *Arundel Deanery*

Incumbent	Patron (where known)

1602   *(impropriator/farmer: Mr Enscourt)*

The coveringe glass windowes and pavinge need mendinge and the walles whitinge

The porch of the chappell is uncovered
the seates neede repairing & planking in the bottom
the [walls] want whiting
the paving wanteth mending
there wanteth allso a convenient pulpitt
there are no bells
the covering and glass windowes need some mending

30 October 1610

The chapell ruynous & there wanteth a preaching pulpett

11 November 1636

There is no Pulpett, nor Carpett, nor Lynnen Cloth for the Communion Table. Both the Church & Chauncell want whiteing & beautifying with Sentences of Scripture.
There is noe Cloth or Cushion for the Pulpett.
They have not the Booke of Homilies nor the Booke for the 5th of November.
The Font will not hould water.
There is noe note indented of the utensills of the Church nor Table of the degrees of marriage.
There [is] noe Surplace for the Minister nor Chest for Alms for the Poore, nor Booke of Canons.
The Church is very darke & wantes to have twoe or three wyndowes more made in it.

Washington – St Mary   *Storrington Deanery*

Incumbent	Patron (where known)
1602 – William Shortred	Magdalen College, Oxford
1610 – William Shortred	
1636 – William Shortred	

1602 [entry very badly torn]
In the [Chauncell] ……..in the ……..are some seates fallen downe under the
eves it [needs] whitinge

The seates are all unborded in the bottomes and lye like graves
the body of the Churche doth want pavinge and the windowes glasinge
the belfry loft is very badly borded it rayneth into the Churche in divers places
the rough cast on the west side the steeple in decay
under the rafte of the vestrie the stoones be downe
the vestry and belfry have no locke and keyes
there are bordes insteede of stones upon the Churche

3 November 1610
The Church wanteth light on the north side the communion table undecent a
buttress on the west end of the vestrie defective the munyons of the west
windowe faultie & the wall on the north end of the Church decayed belowe

6 December 1636
~~The Chauncell is very ruinous both in walling, healing~~, paveing & whiteing &
will fall downe if it ~~be not be speedily repaired. There Chestes stand by the~~
~~Communion Table within~~ the Railes. ~~Some Seates in the Chauncell are much~~
~~deacaied & want reparing. The Parsonage howse is very Ruinous and much~~
~~decaied. The Fence on the North side of the Churchyard is very badd,~~
~~heretofore it was paled, but nowe there is nothing but a bad hedge for the Fence~~
~~hereof, which the Parson~~ ought to doe with pales. Divers other parts of the
Fence of the Churchyard are ~~much in decay & want~~ reparing. They have no
Pulpett cloth. The Communion Table is very old & rotten, they want a new one
more decent & comely. ~~They have noe hoode for the Minister~~, he being a Master
of Artes. The Floore of the Church porch lyeth unpaved & very unseemly.

West Chiltington – St Mary
Storrington Deanery

Incumbent	Patron (where known)
1602 – Robert Johnson	Sir Henry Newell
1610 – Robert Johnson	
1636 – Alan Carr	Alan Carr

1602   *(impropriator/farmer: Robert Johnson)*
The Chauncell wanteth a little glasinge & the walles whitinge

The Churche wanteth a convenient seates to say service in & a comly pulpit
there lacketh some seates, & much pavinge
the walles wante whitinge
one of the bells is broken
the porch on the north side is unborded

3 November 1610
The healing of the south porch faultie the north porch faultie in the ridges & wanteth bordinge

25 November 1636
There are twoe Seats standing on either side in the entrance into the Chauncell under the particion wall which hinder & streighten the passage into the Chauncell.
There are old Chests which stand beside the Communion Table and in equal height with it which ought to be removed.
There is noe Chest for Alms for the poore.
The Ten Comaundments are defaced and Cannot be read.

West Dean – St Andrew   *Boxgrove Deanery*

Incumbent	Patron (where known)
1602 – Joel Wharton	Dean & Chapter
1610 – William Kippes	Thomas Bray
1636 – John Skeppen	William Thomas of Lewes

1602   *(impropriator/farmer: Richard Storey)*

In the Chauncell the pargetinge over the communion table wanteth pavinge & the windowes some pannes of glasse

The Church wanteth some pavinge & healinge
the west dore of the Church is at falte and the walles of the porch

22 October 1610

The porch ill covered at default in coveringe & a cracke in the wall

25 November 1636

The Church wantes to be plaistered & whited throughout.
And the Ten Comaundements & the Kings Armes are to be sett up in the Church.
There wantes a Canopy over the Pulpett.
The Font wantes a better Cover & to be whited.
The Chauncell wantes to be whited & paved.
There is no lynnen Cloth nor Carpett for the Communion Table.
There is no note indented of the Utensills of the Church.
They have noe Booke of Homilies nor Booke of Canons, nor Booke for the 5th of November.
The Plate of the Challice is broken.
There wantes another Flaggon for the Communion wyne & a chest for Almes for the Poore & a ~~hood for the Minister~~. And a Table of the degrees of marriage.
The Church wantes paveing in many places.

West Grinstead – St George   *Storrington Deanery*

Incumbent	Patron (where known)
1602 – Lawrence Bond	Thomas Shirley
1610 – Robert Scott	Bishop of Chichester
1636 – James Hutchinson	Earl of Arundel & Surrey

1602   *(impropriator/farmer: L Bond & T Shirley)*

The Chauncell is a little unpaved and the seates lacke a little mendinge
there is also adioyninge an other Chauncell of Mr Shurlyes which lacketh
pavinge the glas windowes mendinge and the walles whitinge

The Church is very muche at defalte especially in the roofe whereby it rayneth
downe in the Church
the roofe also of the steeple hathe some falte & the walle thereof at one side is
not very good
the [Church] wanteth whiting & bewtifying
the glas windowes mendinge
a great parte of the flower is unpaved

3 November 1610

The Church wanteth pointinge, the coveringe of the steeple below at default,
the font verie undecent a dripp about the west pillar

6 December 1636

~~The Church wantes reparing in the healing thereof in diverse places.~~
The Communion Table is not railed in.
There are divers Seates in the Chauncell standing in equall height with the
Communion Table.
The healing of Mr ~~Step~~ Snelling's Chauncell is in decay & wantes reparing.
Also the seeling of the same Chauncell is much decaied & fallen downe in
divers places.

They want twoe large Flaggons more (beside that which they have already) for the Communion wyne.

The Carpett [of the] Communion Table is very old & hath many holes in it.

Divers of the Seates in the body of the Church are decaied & unboarded in the bottomes & want to be repaired.

There wantes a decent Cover for the Font.

The Church porch is unpaved.

The Fence of the Churchyard is decaied in many places.

West Itchenor – St Nicholas

Boxgrove Deanery

Incumbent	Patron (where known)
1602 – Roger Smith	Crown
1610 – Roger Smith	
1636 – Robert Johnson	

1602

(impropriator/farmer: Roger Smith)

The Chauncell wanteth paving in a place [?]
the wainscote overheade is rotten the windows wolde be scowred and the walls better whited

the Church want paving
the seates be in much decay
the flower which is very rough there pulpit standeth undecently and wanteth a dore there is no 2nd pulpit
the weste dore wanteth locke and key
flower cover is much broken

30 October 1610

The Church wanteth lighte

[November] 1636

To new fenc the Churchyard where yt wantes. A new Carpett for the Communion table and A new flagon for the communion. A chest. The Chest for the poore wantes locks and keies. The Bible is not of the last translation; the book of homilies and A note indented of the utensels of the Church.
To see that the Churchyard is sufficiently railed in with pales; to pave the Church porch; to new white the Church; A new bible of the last translation; to newe bind the service book or buy A new; to pave the Church where it wantes; to repare the Church dore; to see the dunghill in the Churchyard removed; to provide A Clothe for the pullpett and A better Communion table Cloth and to provide A better Cupp for the Communion table

West Stoke – St Andrew   *Boxgrove Deanery*

Incumbent	Patron (where known)
1602 – John Etherington	Crown
1610 – John Etherington	
1636 – Richard Dorrington/	
Walter Whitestones	

1602

The lower seates of the Church neyther paved nor sufficiently repayred
the Churche dore wanteth mendinge and the belfry bordinge

22 October 1610

The steeple is ill covered, a dripp in the north parte of the Church and the
Church wanteth light

25 November 1636

~~The Churchyard wantes to be fenced throughout.~~
~~There is noe Flaggon for the Communion wyne.~~
~~They have not the Booke for the 5th of November,~~ nor a note indented of the
Utensills in the Church.
There is no particion between the Church & Chauncell.
~~There wantes a new Cover for the Font & a new Cloth for the Pulpett.~~
~~Some of the Seats in the Church want paveing.~~
The Bible wantes bindeing.
The Chauncell wantes great reparacions in the Covering.

West Thorney – St Nicholas

Incumbent	Patron (where known)
1602 – Henry Blaxton	Crown
1610 – Godfrey Blaxton	
1636 – Godfrey Blaxton	

1602

(impropriator/farmer: Henry Blaxton)

The Chauncell is not all paved
the windows not all glased
the communion table insufficient
a doore to be provided and the walles
of the saide Chauncel to be mended

The Churche hathe no pavinge at all in
it:
the seats are not decent neither borded
nor planket,
the northe doore to be new mad
a new bell lofte & wheeles for the bells
the steeple to be new poynted and the walles and shingles mended

West Wittering – St Peter and St Paul   *Boxgrove Deanery*

Incumbent	Patron (where known)
1602 – Robert Brinklowe	Prebendary West Wittering
1610 – Robert Brinklowe	
1636 – John Peckham	John Packer & Richard South

18 March 1602 [badly torn]   *(impropriator/farmer: George Osborne)*
The Chauncell wanteth [?] to the upper [?] thereof
the wainscott seates [?] the heade is ruinated
the roofe hath a drippe or two in [the] tyling

The Church wanteth pavinge in the middle and southe iles
the seates are alltogether without pavinge and very rough
the west end south doores wanteth lockes and keyes
the walles of the steeple have one great breache open besides other windowes
whereby it rotteth the timber worke of the bells
the porche wanteth seates and lockes

30 October 1610
The Church wall wanteth pointinge & morteringe, and the eves badly covered,
the south porch ruynated there wanteth a payr of staires to assend up to the
steeple, a buttress on the south side west corner decayed

[November] 1636
There wantes A flagon and ~~A Cupp; the west~~ end to the west end of the
Church to new white the Church

Westbourne – St John the Baptist

Incumbent	Patron (where known)
1602 – Thomas Wilsha	Lord Lumley & Richard Bellingham
1610 – Thomas Wilsha	
1636 – Christopher Swale	Lady Elizabeth Lumley

1602

The Churche wanteth pavinge
the seates bording and the belfry plancking
the walles whitinge within and without to be new poynted
the windowes want glasing
the Churche healing and a new porch to be builded at the south side of the saide Church

25 November 1636

~~There are divers dunghills made in the Churchyard~~.
The parsons Fence against the Churchyard wantes to be better paled.
The Pavement in the Chauncell is suncke in divers places.
Also the Chauncell wantes paling in many places.
The Seates in the Chauncell want repairing.
The Ten Commaundments and ~~the Kings Armes which are sett up in the Church are almost worne out~~.
The Raile about the Communion Table is very slutterly & unseemly.
There wantes a new Carpett for the Communion Table.
~~And a hood for the Minister~~.
There ~~are~~ is noe note indented of the Utensills in the Church.
The belfrey wantes paving.

The Register Booke is not kept in the Church but at the vicars howse.

~~There is no Chest for Almes for the poore.~~

Many Seates in the Church want to be new boarded.

Their Bible is not of the last Translacion.

There wantes a new Cover for the Font.

The Church wantes paving in many places.

Westhampnett – St Peter

Boxgrove Deanery

Incumbent	Patron (where known)
1602 – Thomas Sutton	Toby Langham
1610 – Thomas Sutton	
1636 – William Winche	John Chapman

1602

(impropriator/farmer: Edward Rose)

The Chauncell is decayed in the sealinge and heade
the grounde lyeth unseemly in the pavement
the north side of the Chauncell wanteth poyntinge

The Churche is faltie in healinge, in the glasse windowes in the pavement the
walles the doores the communion table

22 October 1610

The Church ill covered in the north side the Church is darke therefore one of
the north windowes to be inlarged

25 November 1636

The Westend of the Churchyard wantes to be either railed or paled. And part
of the South side wantes the like.
Also the Eastend of the Churchyard wantes the like.
The Church and Chauncell want to be whited throughout, to be adorned with
Sentences of Scripture & the Kinges Arms are to be fairely sett up in the
Church.
There wantes a new Carpett & new lynnen Cloth for the Communion Table.
Some of the seats in the Chancel want planking or paving.
There is not the Booke for the 5th of November.
There wantes a better cloth & Cushion for the Pulpett.
There is no note indented of the utensills of the Church.
Divers Seates in the Church want plancking or paveing.

The Font will not hould water they Christen in a Buckett.

The Chauncell wantes much repaireing in the Covering & the Church wantes Covering in many places.

There is noe Booke of Cannons.

There wantes a new Pulpett the old being very unseemley.

Divers seates in the Church are sunke and want to be raised in many places.

There wantes a flaggon for the Communion wyne.

Wiggonholt – (no known dedication)   *Storrington Deanery*

Incumbent	Patron (where known)
1602 – Richard Boley	
1610 – Richard Boley	
1636 – John Chaloner	

1602   *(impropriator/farmer: Richard Boley)*

The Chauncell wanteth a comely seate
the whole body of the Chauncell is unpaved

There wanteth a convenient seate for the minister to saye service in,
there is noe comly pulpit,
many walles of the Churche are cleven from the toppe to the bottom
the steeple is decayed, it [wyeth?] and hathe shaken downe the sills at the
bottom of it so that it rayneth in to the nether ende of the Churche muche,
the porche is decayed, & bordes are knocked up in steede of tilles
the partition between the Chauncel & the Churche is downe in part,
there wanteth some paving in the boddy of the Churche
there are two seates which a backes behind the Churche dore,
there is a badd seate which wolde be new made, & all the other seates in the
Church are without bottomes of bordes and lye like graves

3 November 1610

the Church porch the communion table the south dore & the font all much
decayed

25 November 1636

The Fence of the Churchyard is very much at default in divers places round
about the Church so that hoggs come in and much annoy the Churchyard.
The Church porch is very ruynous & like to fall downe, the sills being suncke
away and almost quite consumed.
The Church is also unpaved and the flower hereof lyeth very uneven &
undecent.

The Flaggon for the Communion Wyne is unfitt & unseemly, being like an Alehouse quart pott.

There are Seates and forms which stand in the Chauncell in equal height with the Communion Table.

They want a better book of Common Praier that which they have is old and imperfect.

The Register Book is not kept in the Chest in the Church according to the Canon but is kept in the Parsons howse.

They have noe Chest for Almes for the poore.

They have noe Table of the degrees of marriage.

The Font is at default and will not hold water.

Wisborough Green – St Peter ad Vincula

Storrington Deanery

Incumbent	Patron (where known)
1602 – Christopher Butler	George Turner
1610 – Christopher Butler	
1636 – Christopher Butler	

1602
(impropriator/farmer: Matthew Napper)

The Chauncell wanteth some shingles in the healing

The healinge over the Churche is some iii or iv places in defalte
the windowes want glasse
the steeple wanteth shingles
the seates most parte unplancked

6 December 1636

They have noe Flaggon for the Communion wyne but a glasse Botle wherein they fetch the wyne from the Taverne.
The Pavement above the Raile in the Chauncell is to be amended & levelled.
They have noe Chest for Almes for the poore but have a hole in the Chest wherein the Register Booke is kept whereinto they putt the Almes for the poore when any are given.
They have noe Cloth for the Pulpett & their cushion is very old & worne out & not fit for that use.

Wiston – St Michael   *Storrington Deanery*

Incumbent	Patron (where known)
1602 – John Bingham	Sir Thomas Shirley
1610 – Daniel Price	
1636 – William Stannard	Ann Shirley (widow)

1602   *(impropriator/farmer: John Bingham)*

The partition between the Church and Chauncell is not very good and decent

The Church seates some of them are very badd
the flower in some places is unpaved
it hathe but two bells and the one of them is broken

3 November 1610

To certify faults & repair

25 November 1636

The Earle of Thannettes Chauncell is uncovered and wantes repairing and whiteing.
The Parrish Chauncell hath some defect in the ~~healing~~ seeling & pavement & also wantes new whiteing.
They want a bigger and fairer Flaggon for the Communion Wyne.
They have not the Booke of Canons nor Table of the degrees of marriage.
Divers seats in the Church & Chauncell are much in decay in many places.
The Font is in decay & will not hold water, so that the Minister is forced to baptise in a bason.

Woolavington – St Peter

Midhurst Deanery

Incumbent	Patron (where known)
1602 – Henry Stoughton	Earl of Arundel
1610 – Daniel German	Crown
1636 – Daniel German	

1602

The Churche wanteth whitinge
the pavinge is much decayed in the Churche especially in the nether ende
the seates are all ruinouse in the southe side
the steeple is very ruinous
the porch is at reparacyons

3 November 1610

The shingle of the steeple much decayed the roofe of the Church ruynous & decayed and the belframe altogether rotten

25 November 1636

Some part of the Church is like to fall downe if it be not speedily amended.
The Foundacion of the Church porch is suncke.
The Church porch wantes to be all new paved.
They have not the Servyce Booke for the 5th of November.
The wall of the Steeple is like to fall downe.
They have noe note indented of the utensills of the Church.
The Churchyard lyeth very fowle & there lyeth a dung heap on the North side of the Chauncell wall.

Woolbeding – All Saints   *Midhurst Deanery*

Incumbent	Patron (where known)
1602 – Guy Dobbins	Edmund Gray
1610 – Edmund Gray	Thomas Gray
1636 – Edmund Gray	

1602   *(impropriator/farmer: Thomas Gray)*
The healinge walles glass windowes pavinge & seates in the Chauncell at defecte

The ridging, walles glas windowes, at some defect
ii or iii of the seates to be repaired
many of the other of the seates want flowrynge
the pavinge broken & the Churche porche to be better flowered & inclosed

25 November 1636
The Church porch wantes paveing.
There is a Chest in the Chauncell which stands in equall height with the
Communion Table.
There wantes a new Communion Booke.
They Christen Children in a Bason because the Font will not hold water.
The Ten Commaundments & the Kings Armes want to be fairly sett up &
Sentences of Scripture in the Church.
There wantes a new Communion Table.
There is a seat on the South side of the Chauncell which wantes paveing.
The rest of the Seates in the Church are decaied & want reparing.
They want a Flaggon or a potle for the Communion wyne.
There wantes a new Pulpett & a more Convenient seat for the Minister.
The Pulpett standeth even with the reading place.
They want ~~they~~ the Service Booke for the 5th of November.
They have noe note indented of the utensills of the Church.

Yapton – St Mary   *Arundel Deanery*

Incumbent	Patron (where known)
1602 – Hugh Roberts	Crown
1610 – Hugh Roberts	
1636 – Anthony Hilton	Bishop of Chichester

1602   *(impropriator/farmer: Walter Edmonds)*

The steeple to be made even and the whole Church to be paved
the seates are to be made

The Churche is to be paved in many places
all the three dores are insufficient
the steeple greatly needeth reparacion
the seates are not seemly
the walls are not bewtified with sentences of scripture but deformed with grip
[gower?] made by the mason

30 October 1610

The steeple verie ruynous & must be newe built the post of the porch rotten, &
there wanteth [a reading pul – crossed out] a preaching pulpett

25 November 1636

The Church Porch wantes to be paved.
The Chauncell wantes to be whited & adorned with Scripture.
There is noe Booke of homilies, nor Table of the degrees of marriage nor note
indented of the utensills of the Church; the kings Armes which were sett up in
the Church are almost worne out.
The Seates in the Church are much decaied.
The Rayle about the Communion Table is too little.
The Church wantes paveing in very many places.
There wantes a better Cloth & Cushion for the Pulpett.
They have not the Service Booke for the 5th of November nor a note indented
of the Utensills of the Church.
There wantes a new Cover for the Font.

Fishbourne – St Peter and St Mary   *The Dean of Chichester's Peculiar*

Incumbent	Patron (where known)
1602 – Edward Bragge	Crown
1610 – Edward Bragge/Francis Cox	
1636 – Thomas Hooke	

1602

In the Chancell
The paving is decayed.
The wales be decayed & not whited.
The seates be decayed & not borded.
The windowes be decayed & darke.
The rofe is decayed.
The table of the Ten Commandments is woren out.
There is no convenient seat for the minister.

In the Body of the Church
The particion is decayed and not at all bewtified.
The seates be all unborded.
There be two seates much decayed.
The ffont wants some repayre.
The pulpet is much decayed and stands not as it ought.
The Communion table hath not of the furniture as it ought.
The windowes would be new glased.
The wales be not whited.
There is no Sentences of Scripture written.
The west end of the Church is unpaved.
The coming into the Church is much decayed.
The Church porch is much decayed.

Rumboldswhyke – St Mary   *The Dean of Chichester's Peculiar*

Incumbent	Patron (where known)
1602 – Godfrey Blaxton	Dean & Chapter
1610 – William Cox	
1636 – John Taylor/ Robert Randall	

1602

In the Chancell
Half the Chancell is unpaved.
There is no seates in it.
The wales are neyther repayred nor whited.
The glasse windowes are decayed.
The rofe is decayed.
The table of the Tenn Commandments is decayed.
The seat for the minister is not decent.

In the Body of the Church
There is no particion between the Chauncell & the Church.
The pulpit doth want a dore.
The seates are not borded.
The Font is altogether decayed.
The seates next the Church dore are very undecent.
The Church is not paved at the west end.
The west end of the Church is made rather a storehouse than a place of prayer.

St Andrew Chichester   *The Dean of Chichester's Peculiar*

Incumbent	Patron (where known)
1602 – Thomas Leame	Dean & Chapter
1610 – John Meade	
1636 – Robert Johnson	

1602

In the Chauncell
The seates ar much decayed &
unborded.
The wales be very fowle.
The windowes much broken.
There is no table on the
Commandements.

In the body of the Church
The particion is very fowle & ruinous.
The paving be decayed.
The seates are very bad & all unborded.
The wales be very fowle.
The ont is much decayed.
The Communion table hath very bad furniture.
There is no Sentences of Scripture written on the wales.
The dore at the west end of the Church is very rotten.
The west end of the Church lieth
very undecently within.
The Church porch is ready to fall
downe.

St Bartholomew Chichester   *The Dean of Chichester's Peculiar*

Incumbent	Patron (where known)
1602 – Nicholas Wood	Dean and Chapter
1610 – Nicholas Wood	
1636 – William Chandler	

1602

In the Chauncell
The seates ar very bad.
The wales be very fowle.
The table of the Commandements is woren out.

In the body of the Church
The seates be much decayed.
The wales be very fowle.
The glasse windowes be decayed.
The Font is much decayed.
The Communion table hath not decent furniture.
There is noe Sentences of Scripture written in the Church.
The sealing is falen downe and the Chauncell dore is much decayed.
The Church porch is much decayed.

27 October 1610

Our Church is somewhat at defaulte

St Martin Chichester   *The Dean of Chichester's Peculiar*

Incumbent	Patron (where known)
1602 – Anthony Buttery	Dean & Chapter
1610 – Anthony Hopwood	
1636 – William Winche	

1602

In the Chauncell
The seates are very bad.
The wales are very fowle.
The windowes are very darke.
The Commandements are decayed.

In the body of the Church
The particion is very bad.
The pavings are much decayed.
The seates are very ruinous and
unborded.
The wales are very fowle.
The Font is much decayed.
The Church is much annoyed with a
poundfold mayde against the Church
wale.

St Olave Chichester   *The Dean of Chichester's Peculiar*

Incumbent	Patron (where known)
1602 – Valentine Austen	Dean & Chapter
1610 – John Guy	
1636 – Robert Johnson	

1602

In the Chauncell
The wales are very ruinous and crackt in
many places from the top to the bottom & the
wales be very fowle.
The glasse windowes be very dark.
The Ten Commandements written on the wall
are woren out.
The rofe is very fowle & decayed.
The pavings ar in divers places decayed.
The seates are broken downe.

In the Body of the Church
The particion is not bewtified as it ought.
The wales be very fowle.
The Font is decayed.
The Communion table hath not his furniture
either decently or orderly.

27 October 1610

The steeple of our Church is somewhat
decayed for want of covering we have not a
bible of the new translation we have not
hitherto wrote the names of those that have
bin absent uppon the Sundayes or holy dayes
from divine service

St Pancras Chichester   *The Dean of Chichester's Peculiar*

Incumbent	Patron (where known)
1602 – John Lilliott	Dean & Chapter
1610 – John Lilliott	
1636 – William Speed	George Oglander

1602

In the Chauncell
The glasse windowes be somewhat decayed.
Mr W [M]oore hath bilt a seate in the Chancell neyther comly nor orderly.

In the body of the Church
The partition is very bad & much decayed.
The Communion table is not furnished as it ought to be.
Theare is no Sentences of Scripture written on the wales.
Many of the seates be unborded & much decayed.
It is not paved in many places.
The Font is decayed.
The Churchwardens doe lay both lime & sand in the Church and make morter
by the Font which makes it very fowle.
The porch is much decayed.

27 October 1610

Our Churchyard is not well fenced by reason yt is to be done by my Lord Bpp
and to specifie the names of those that refuse to send their children to the
Minister

St Peter the Great Chichester (Subdeanery)   *The Dean of Chichester's Peculiar*

Incumbent	Patron (where known)
1602 – George Payne	Crown
1610 – George Payne	
1636 – John Payne	Augustine Hitchcock, Alderman of Chichester

1602

In the Chauncell
The wales in the Chauncell be very foule.
The glasse windowes be very darke & muche decayed.
The pavinge is decayed.
The partition is not as it ought to be.

In the body of the Church
The Churchwardens have removed certayne seates and place then very
unorderly, & the places where the old seates did stand is left very foule &
unpaved.
Many seates be unborded and much decayed & all the seates generally so fouly
kept & ruenated as is noe way convenient for any people to sitt in.
The font is very ill kept & undecently ordered
The Communion table wants both convenient covering and hath a very bad
lynen clothe on it and without any choyse.
The pulpett is a very bad one.
The Church is most fowly kept by the Clarke.

27 October 1610

The glass windowes from our parish Church are much decayed which ought to
be mended by the Deane and Chapter there is likewise lacking a pullpitt clothe
and cushion & carpet with a lynnen cloth to cover the communion table and a
table of the degrees of marriage there is likewise wantinge a silver or pewter
pott for the communion

St Peter the Less Chichester   *The Dean of Chichester's Peculiar*

Incumbent	Patron (where known)
1602 – William Lawes	Crown
1610 – John Guy	
1636 – John Guy	

1602

In the Chauncell
The pavinge be decayed
There is a seat for Mr Chatfield so
neare the Communion table as doth
obscure the same very much.
There is another seat wheare Mr
Palmer sett a verye bad one.

In the body of the Church
There be divers seates very much decayed & the Churchwardens have been
warned to have them amended but they will not doe it & all the seates in the
Church be unborded.
The wales be very ill kept, & no Sentences of Scripture is written one them.
The Communion table wants decent lynnen for this furniture.
One the Southside of the Church the rofe is very undecent and ought to be
repayred.
Divers places be unpaved in the Church.
The Church porch is much decayed.
The frame of the bells is very much decayed & the steeple also.
The stayres to the Roode loft would be defaced.

27 October 1610

[parson's presentment of the Churchwardens]
They omitted to present themselves for not having a book of homilies and
likewise the Church windowes at the easte end are in decaye and want
reparacions in glassinge and the body of the Church about the font in pavinge
they have no pulpitt and the font is at fault and will hold no water as yt ought
but they sett a basin therein to baptize withall they have neere a book of
Canons neyther yett any book of prayers sett out for the King's deliverance to
be used yerely the fifth of November forever

All Saints Chichester

Peculiar of Pagham and Tarring

Incumbent	Patron (where known)
1602 – Robert Taylor	Archbishop of Canterbury
1610 – Anthony Hopwood	
1636 – Joshua Petoe or Peyto	

18 January 1603

The bodie of the Church some of the
pavements are broken upp & not
amended

the west dore is decayed

the seats are not borded nor floored in
the bottoms

the healing and the glasse windows are
at some falte and the walles within are
not whited.

Bersted – St Mary Magdalene   *Peculiar of Pagham and Tarring*

Incumbent	Patron (where known)
1602 – Robert Evans	Archbishop of Canterbury
1610 – Geoffrey More	
1636 – Mauice Rowland	

14 January 1603

The bodie of the Church hath in it divers [?] the healing at falte.

The partition betweene the Chancell & the bodie of the Church is very ruinous.

The pavement under foote is greatly broken up and decayed

the seats for the west parte are utterlie decayed and neither borded floored nor paved in the bottomes and marvelous undecent inconvenient for the people.

The south dore wanteth some amendment and the glasse windows are greatly decayed and some of them stopped up and overgrown with vine.

Durrington

Peculiar of Pagham and Tarring

Incumbent	Patron (where known)
	Archbishop of Canterbury

18 January 1603

The Chancell is unpaved and lyeth very badly
the glass windows and the healing at falte [wainscot] seates and partition is decayed.

The pavement in the bodie of the Church is broken up
the seates are not floored
The porch and the north dore are sumwhatt at falte and must be amended and the walles on the inside are not whited.

East Lavant – St Mary   *Peculiar of Pagham and Tarring*

Incumbent	Patron (where known)
1602 – Garrett Williamson	Archbishop of Canterbury
1610 – Martin Okin	
1636 – Owen Stockton/Joseph Henshaw	

11 February 1603

In the bodie of the Church the pavements are broken upp

the healing is at some falte

the west dore is decayed and the seates are decayed and some of them are unfloored

the glasses is not clean which doth greatly darken the Church and the walles are not whited

also the steeple wanteth a buttresse for the stay thereof.

Heene – St Botolph

Peculiar of Pagham and Tarring

Incumbent	Patron (where known)
	Archbishop of Canterbury

18 January 1603

The south Chancell is thatched with straw

the glass windows are decayed and many of them darbed up with earth and there wants a convenient seate for the minister

the Church seats are decayed and lye very badly neither borded nor floored in the bottoms

the south dore must be new made and the healing and the porch wanteth some amendment

the pavements are broken and decayed

the walles within not whited but stand in very undecent manner.

The Chancel where the communion table standeth is all unpaved and unfloored

the healing is at falte

the partition in the Chancel and the wainscot seats and the wainscot overhead are decayed and the walles of the Chancel are not whited.

Pagham – St Thomas à Becket

Peculiar of Pagham and Tarring

Incumbent	Patron (where known)
1602 – Henry Harrison	Archbishop of Canterbury
1610 – Edward Bangor	
1636 – Edward Bangor	

11 February 1603

The glass windows bodie of the Church wanteth some amendment in the heling

[?...] of the pavements hath been broken uppe and are not amended but lye very ruinously

The seates for the moste parte are mightelie decayed and are neither borded paved not floored in the bottomes and lye in greater disorder

the south dore is at falte and the south porch hathe bine taken downe of late and is not rectified

The glass windows are somewhat decayed and the walles within are not whited there hath some lead been taken down from the steeple of late but there hath bine shingle substantially layed upp in the place thereof.

The west dore and north dore want some amendment

Patching – St John the Divine

Peculiar of Pagham and Tarring

Incumbent	Patron (where known)
1602 – George Goldman	Archbishop of Canterbury
1610 – David English	
1636 – Walter Whitestones	

14 January 1603

our steeple shalbe done so sone as conveniently we can do it

18 January 1603

The steeple not hilded since the tempest overthrew it

the porch and the north dore are at falte

the pavement and the seates in the bodie of the Church are also decayed

some of the glass windows are not yet amended

Slindon – St Mary   *Peculiar of Pagham and Tarring*

Incumbent	Patron (where known)
1602 – Francis Cox	Gerard Kempe of Slindon
1610 – Francis Cox	
1636 – William Ford	

14 January 1603

The bodie of the Church there wants a convenient seate for the Minister and the pulpit is also at falte.

The seates and pavements of the bodie of the Church are greatly decayed and do be very ruinously

the healing and glass windows are at falte

the south doore wanteth some mending and the Church walles within are not whited.

Tangmere – St Andrew

Peculiar of Pagham and Tarring

Incumbent	Patron (where known)
1602 – Henry Ball	Henry Hodgson/ Henry Walrond
1610 – Robert Tayer	Cecil Harrison
1636 – Francis Heath	Crown

11 February 1603

The bodie of the Church wants a convenient pulpit
the pavements and seates are at falte
the steeple and porch want some bording and the walles are not whited within.

Tarring – St Andrew   *Peculiar of Pagham and Tarring*

Incumbent	Patron (where known)
1602 – Martin Williams/ Benjamin Carrier	Archbishop of Canterbury
1610 – Benjamin Carrier	
1636 – Samuel Barnard	

18 January 1603

in the Chancel there lacketh some
amendment in the healing and glasse
windows
The pavements in some parts are at
falte
the wainscott overhead wanteth some
amendment and some of the wainscott
seates wants bordes in the bottomes
the walles within are not whiteth.

The communion table is not comely
the bodie of the Church hath the healing at falte
the pavement wants some amendment in divers places
the seats are something decayed and all unborded in the bottomes
the glass windowes are at falte & the glass so eaten with cancre that it darkneth
the Church very muche
the south dore wanteth amendment and the walles within are not whited
which also causeth the darke Church to be darker.

APPENDIX 1:
ARCHBISHOP WHITGIFT'S LETTER TO HIS BISHOPS CALLING FOR A SURVEY OF CHURCHES

Salutem in Christ: Her Majestie being enformed that divers churches and chauncells within this realme are greatlie decayed and some of them either falne downe or lyke to fall downe and likewise that many other churches be very ondecentlie kepte within to the disgrace of Religion, and great offence to many well disposed, and occasion to such as are enymies to our profession to thincke that wee are but prophanlye mynded and without devotion; Haithe commanded me to write to the Archbishop of Yorke for his province and to all the Bpps within my province, in her name to charge them to have spetiall regard to the premises and to take care that the same bee reformed accordinglie which hereby I notifie unto your Lordship [in this case the Bishop of Lincoln]. And require yow in her Majestie's name to see the same duly performed and reformed as yow will aunswer to the contrary, and to certifie me in convenient tyme the state of the churches within your Diocese. And what you have done concerning the same. And soe with my hartie commendacians, I committee your Lordship to the tuicion of the Almightie God;

ffrom Lambeth this xxi of June 1602
Your loving brother in Christe, Jo: Cantuar

Foster, C.W., ed., The State of the Church, Vol I, Lincolnshire Record Society, 23, 1926, 220.

The Judge and Registrar received this letter on 4 July 1602 following which a survey of the archdeaconries of Lincoln and Stowe was conducted and the results sent to the Bishop of Lincoln on 20 September 1602.

APPENDIX 2:
TIMESCALE PERTINENT TO THE SURVEY OF 1602-3

21 June 1602:

Archbishop Whitgift wrote to his bishops requesting a survey of churches and chapels throughout the land to be carried out for each archdeaconry (Appendix 1).

September 1602:

The first Sussex church surveys were recorded as churchwardens and impropriators, or their farmers, appeared in Chichester before a judge and a notary, and were then given dates by which they should certify that repairs had been carried out, which was, in most cases, by Easter of the following year (Ep. I/26/1).

September – December 1602:

The vast majority of surveys were completed in sessions copied up into a separate detection book (Ep.I/26/1).

January – February – March 1603:

Reports were given on the 9 churches of the Dean of Chichester's Peculiar (Ep. III/6/Box 407/folder 3/25) and the 10 churches of the Archbishop of Canterbury's Peculiar of Pagham and Tarring (Ep. IV/2/8, ff.22r-24v).

May 1603:

A large number of churches and chapels were signed off as hoped for at Easter (see Appendix 5).

30 June 1603:

Archbishop Whitgift asked his clergy to supply details regarding numbers of communicants, recusants, pluralities and impropriations in a further effort to find out more about the state of the Church of England on the accession of James VI & I, and to allay Puritan criticisms of the Church reported in the Millenary Petition (Appendix 3).

August-September 1603:

Bishop Watson conducted his triennial visitation of the diocese of Chichester (see appendix 4 for the questions he had asked about churches on his earlier visitation in 1600).

February 1604:

The Hampton Court Conference was convened to discuss the state of the Church of England following criticisms made by Puritans; it was presided over by King James VI and I, an unusual step that boosted the hopes of Puritans and must have given some of his bishops palpitations. It proved to be something of a disaster for evangelical reformers, but it did lead to the publication of the King James Authorised Version of the Bible in 1611. Several people associated with Chichester helped with the writing of this great work: Lancelot Andrewes, Roger Andrewes and William Thorne.

March 1604:

Eight Sussex churches were still in the process of getting work signed off in the last court meeting recorded in Ep. I/26/1: Broadwater, East Preston, Earnley, Birdham, Stoughton, Kirdford, Bramber & Upmarden.

March-July 1604:

Convocation drew up 141 Canons that were accepted by the King and promulgated as the laws of the Church of England (see Appendix 6 for the canons concerning care of churches and what they were expected to contain).

APPENDIX 3:
ARCHBISHOP WHITGIFT'S ARTICLES TO HIS BISHOPS OF 30 JUNE 1603[147]

After my hartye commendations greeting.

The matters I nowe desire to be advertized with all convenient speed are these:

1. The certaine number of those that doe receive the communion in everie several parishe.

2. The certain number of everie man recusant inhabiting in every severall parishe within your severall Jurisdictions without specifyinge their particular names; and likewyse the certain number of every woman recusant distinct from the men in manner as aforesayd.

3. The like enquirie to be observed to note what the certyn number is, of everie man as afore whoe doth not receive the communion, as also the certayne number of every woman in each severall parishe who doth not receive the communion without specifying their names.

4. The particular name of every double beneficed man in your Dioces who holdeth two benefices with Cure; his degree of Schoole and qualification; the name of the severall benefices with Cure which he soe holdeth; howe many miles distance each of the benefices which he soe holdeth is from the other; And as nere as you can the valuation of them in the Kings bookes.

5. Howe many severall impropriations there be within your Diocese; whether they be indued with vicaridges or served by curates; yf with vicarydges what every of those severall vicaridges is valued at as nere as you can inform yourself in the Kinge's Bookes; yf by curates what the ordinary stipend is that the impropriator payeth for the maintenance of the curate.

6. The name of every parsonage within your Diocese which is indued with a vicaridge; what the [sayd] parsonage is valued [at] in the Kinge's bookes; and what the vicaridge is valued at.

7. Who is patron to each severall benefice within your Dioces soe nere as your recorde of Institutions can giev direction.

And thus praying your L. to be very careful in the premisses I comitt to you in the protection of Almightie God. From Lambeyth this last day of June 1603.
Your Lo[rdshi]ps loving brother in Christ. J.C.

---

[147] Transcript used by W.C.Renshaw, *Ecclesiastical Returns for 81 Parishes in East Sussex, SRS,* IV, 1905, 4.

APPENDIX 4:
EXTRACT FROM VISITATION ARTICLES OF BISHOP ANTHONY WATSON, 1600

Touching the place of Common Praier in the Church

1   Whether the Chauncell, Church and Chappell bee sufficiently repaired as well in stone, timber, lead, tyle, glasse, as all other necessary things & if they bee not, through whose default this is omitted.

2   Whether your Churchyard bee sufficiently fenced and decently kept, & the trees therein growing not spoiled.

3   Whether the walles of the Church bee within whited, & beautified with fruitfull sentences of scripture out of the holy Scriptures; and paved comely in the bodie of the Church & the Chancell.

4   Whether you have in your parish Church & Chappell, all thinges necessarie for the setting forth of common praier and administration of the Sacraments, namely the booke of Common Praier, two psalters in prose and meeter: the English Bible in the largest volume, which is now authorized by consent of the Bishops of this Realme: the two tomes of Homelies: the Paraphrases of Erasmus in English: the table of the ten Commandements of God: a convenient Pulpit well placed, a decent table standing on a frame, for the holy Communion, with a faire linnen cloth to lay upon the same, and some covering of silk, buccharam, or other such like, for the keeping cleane thereof, a comely Communion Cup of silver with a cover of silver for the same, which may serve for the administration of the Communion Bread: a decent Surplus with large sleeves: a Register booke in parchment of Christnings, weddings, & burials: a sure cofer with three lockes & keies for the keeping of the said register booke.

5   Whether all monuments of superstition bee defaced and cleane removed: as Altars, Rewdeloftes, Copes, Westments, holy water, stockes, images, and all popish bookes either Latine or English.

6   Whether you have a Clarke, Sexton, or decon to asist your priest dutifully in reading the psalmes, first lesson, the Epistle, and such other services: & also to keep the bookes and ornaments of the Church, the Church it selfe, the quier, the Communion table, the Pulpit & the Font, faire cleane and decent, against the time of service of the Communion, Sermon and Baptisme, and by whom he be chosen.

APPENDIX 5:
ALPHABETICAL LIST OF CHURCHES AND REPAIR WORK UNDERTAKEN BY 1603

Parish	chancel	church
Aldingbourne	June 1603	1 Oct 1603
Amberley	No certificate	[late] Oct 1603
Angmering	No certificate	May 1603
Appledram	May 1603	May 1603
Arundel	May 1603	May 1603
Ashurst	Excommunication	May 1603
Barlavington	No certificate	No certificate
Barnham	May 1603	May 1603
Bepton	May 1603	May 1603
Bignor	No certificate	May 1603
Billingshurst	No certificate	May 1603
Binsted	May 1603	May 1603
Birdham	No certificate	[-] March 1603/4
Bosham	14 Dec 1603	May 1603
Botolphs	May 1603	May 1603
Boxgrove	May 1603	May 1603
Bramber	No certificate	May 1603
Broadwater	No certificate	1 Oct 1603
Burpham	May 1603	May 1603
Bury	May 1603	No certificate
Chidham	May 1603	May 1603
Chiltington	May 1603	May 1603
Chithurst	May 1603	1 Oct 1603
Clapham	No certificate	June 1603
Climping	May 1603	1 Oct 1603 certified as not repaired
Cocking	No certificate	May 1603
[Coldwaltham?]	No record	May 1603
Combes	No certificate	No certificate
Compton	May 1603	May 1603 & [late] Oct 1603
Didling	May 1603	No certificate
Donnington	Excommunication	May 1603

ALPHABETICAL LIST OF CHURCHES AND REPAIR WORK (cont)		
Parish	chancel	church
Earnley	No certificate	May 1603
Eartham	May 1603	14 Dec 1603
Easebourne	May 1603	May 1603
East Dean	June 1603	June 1603
East Marden	No certificate	May 1603
East Preston	No certificate	No certificate
East Wittering	No certificate	May 1603
Eastergate	No certificate	May 1603
Elsted	May 1603	May 1603
Felpham	June 1603	June 1603
Fernhurst	May 1603	May 1603
Ferring	No certificate	No certificate
Findon	No certificate	June 1603
Fittleworth	Excommunication	June 1603
Ford	May 1603	May 1603
Funtington	14 Dec 1603	May 1603
G[reatham?]	May 1603	May 1603
Goring	No certificate	May 1603
Graffham	No certificate	No certificate
Harting	No certificate	May 1603
Herringham (Hardham)	May 1603	May 1603
Heyshott	No certificate	May 1603
Horsham	No certificate	No certificate
Houghton	May 1603	May 1603
Hunston	May 1603	May 1603
Iping	May 1603	May 1603
Itchingfield	No certificate	No certificate
Kingston	No certificate	10 Dec 1603
Kirdford	No certificate	No certificate
Lancing	May 1603	May 1603
Linchmere	May 1603	May 1603
Littlehampton	May 1603	May 1603
Lodsworth	May 1603	May 1603
Lurgashall	May 1603	May 1603
Lyminster	May 1603	May 1603

ALPHABETICAL LIST OF CHURCHES AND REPAIR WORK (cont)		
Parish	*chancel*	*church*
Madehurst	May 1603	No certificate
Merston	May 1603	May 1603
Mid Lavant	May 1603	No certificate
Middleton	No certificate	May 1603
Midhurst	No certificate	May 1603
Norrth Stoke	May 1603	May 1603
North Marden	May 1603	May 1603
Nuthurst	June 1603	1 Oct 1603
Oving	No certificate	May 1603
Parham	No certificate	May 1603
Poling	May 1603	May 1603
Racton	May 1603	May 1603
Rudgwick	May 1603	May 1603
Rusper	No certificate	May 1603
Rustington	May 1603	1 Oct 1603
Selham	No certificate	No certificate
Selsey	10 Dec 1603	10 Dec 1603
Shipley	May 1603	May 1603
Sidlesham	May 1603	May 1603
Singleton	May 1603	May 1603
Slinfold	May 1603	May 1603
South Stoke	May 1603	May 1603
Stedham	May 1603	May 1603
Steyning	No certificate	No certificate
Storrington	No certificate	No certificate
Stoughton	No certificate	June 1603
Sullington	No certificate	May 1603
Sutton	No certificate	May 1603
Thakeham	No certificate	May 1603
Tillington	No certificate	June 1603
Tortington	May 1603	May 1603
Treyford	1 Oct 1603	May 1603
Trotton	May 1603	May 1603
Tuxlith	May 1603	May 1603
Up Marden	May 1603	No certificate

ALPHABETICAL LIST OF CHURCHES AND REPAIR WORK (cont)		
Parish	*chancel*	*church*
Up Waltham	May 1603	May 1603
Walberton	May 1603	May 1603
Warminghurst	May 1603	May 1603
Warnham	June 1603	June 1603
Warningcamp	No certificate	No certificate
Washington	No certificate	10 Dec 1603
West Dean	May 1603	May 1603
West Dean Binderton	May 1603	May 1603
West Dean Chilgrove	May 1603	
West Grinstead	No certificate	No certificate
West Itchenor	No certificate	May 1603
West Stoke	May 1603	May 1603
West Thorney	No certificate	May 1603
West Wittering	No certificate	May 1603
Westbourne	May 1603	May 1603
Westhampnett	May 1603	May 1603
Wiggonholt	May 1603	May 1603
Wisborough Green	No certificate	May 1603
Wiston	No certificate	1 Oct 1603
Woolbeding	May 1603	May 1603
Woollavington	No certificate	May 1603
Yapton	May 1603	June 1603

APPENDIX 6:
EXTRACT FROM THE CANONS OF 1604: THINGS APPERTAINING TO CHURCHES

80   The great Bible and book of common prayer to be had in every church.
The churchwardens or questmen of every church and chapel shall, at the
charge of the parish, provide the book of common prayer, lately explained in
some few points by his majesty's authority according to the laws and his
highness's prerogative in that behalf, and that with all convenient speed, but at
the furthest within two months after the publishing of these our constitutions.
And if any parishes be yet unfurnished of the Bible of the largest volume, or of
the books of homilies allowed by Authority, the said churchwardens shall
within convenient time provide the same at the like charge of the parish.

81   A font of stone for baptism in every church.
According to a former constitution, too much neglected in many places, we
appoint, That there shall be a font of stone in every church and chapel where
baptism is to be ministered; the same to be set in the ancient usual places, in
which only font the minister shall baptize publicly.

82   A decent communion table in every church.
Whereas we have no doubt, but that in all churches within the realm of
England, convenient and decent tables are provided and placed for the
celebration of the holy communion, we appoint that the same tables shall from
time to time be kept and repaired in sufficient and seemly manner, and
covered in time of divine service with a carpet of silk or other decent stuff,
thought meet by the ordinary of the place, if any question be made of it, and
with a fair linen cloth at the time of the ministration, as becometh that table,
and so stand, saving when the said holy communion is to be administered: at
which time the same shall be placed in so good sort within the church or
chancel as thereby the minister may be more conveniently heard of the
communicants in his prayer and administration, and the communicants also
more conveniently and in more number, may communicate with the said
minister: and that the ten commandments be set up on the east end of every
church and chapel where the people may best see and read the same, and other
chosen sentences written upon the walls of the said churches and chapels in
places convenient: And likewise, that a convenient seat be made for the
minister to read service in. All these to be done at the charge of the parish.

83   A pulpit to be provided in every church.
The churchwardens or questmen, at the common charge of the parishioners in
every church, shall provide a comely and decent pulpit, to be set in a
convenient place within the same, by the discretion of the ordinary of the

place, if any question do arise, and to be there seemly kept for the preaching of God's Word.

84 A chest for alms in every church.

The churchwardens shall provide and have, within three months after the publishing of these constitutions, a strong chest with a hole in the upper part thereof, to be provided at the charge of the parish (if there be none such already provided) having three keys, of which one shall remain in the custody of the parson, vicar, or curate, and the other two in the custody of the churchwardens for the time being; which chest they shall set and fasten in the most convenient place, to the intent the parishioners may put into it their alms for their poor neighbours. And the parson, vicar, or curate shall diligently from time to time, and especially when men make their testaments, call upon, exhort, and move their neighbours to confer, and give as they may well spare, to the said chest; declaring unto them that whereas heretofore they have been diligent to bestow much substance otherwise than God commanded, upon superstitious uses, now they ought at this time to be much more ready to help the poor and needy, knowing that to relieve the poor is a sacrifice which pleaseth God; and that also whatsoever is given for their comfort is given to Christ himself, and is so accepted of him that he will mercifully reward the same. The which alms and devotion of the people, the keepers of the keys shall yearly, quarterly, or oftener (as need requireth), take out of the chest, and distribute the same in the presence of most of the parish, or six of the chief of them, to be truly and faithfully delivered to their most poor and needy neighbours.

85 Churches to be kept in sufficient reparations.

The churchwardens or questmen shall take care, and provide that the churches be well and sufficiently repaired, and so from time to time kept and maintained, that the windows be well glazed, and that the floors be kept paved, plain, and even, and all things there in such an orderly and decent sort, without dust, or any thing that may be either noisome or unseemly, as best becometh the house of God, and is prescribed in an homily to that effect. The like care they shall take, that the churchyards be well and sufficiently repaired, fenced and maintained with walls, rails, or pales, as have been in each place accustomed at their charges unto whom by law the same appertaineth: but especially they shall see that in every meeting of the congregation, peace be well kept, and that all persons excommunicated, and so denounced, be kept out of the church.

86 Churches to be surveyed, and the decays certified to the high commissioners.

Every dean, dean and chapter, archdeacon, and others which have authority to hold ecclesiastical visitations by composition, law, or prescription, shall survey the churches of his or their jurisdiction, once in every three years in his own person, or cause the same to be done, and shall from time to time within the said three years, certify the high commissioners for causes ecclesiastical, every year, of such defects in any the said churches, as he or they do find to remain unrepaired, and the names and surnames of the parties faulty therein. Upon which certificate, we desire that the said high commissioners will ex officio mero send for such parties, and compel them to obey the just and lawful decrees of such ecclesiastical ordinaries making such certificates.

87 A terrier of glebe-lands and other possessions belonging to churches.

We ordain that the archbishops and all bishops within their several dioceses shall procure (as much as in them lieth) that a true note and terrier of all the glebes, lands, meadows, gardens, orchards, houses, stocks, implements, tenements, and portions of tythes, lying out of their parishes (which belong to any parsonage, or vicarage, or rural prebend) be taken by the view of honest men in every parish, by the appointment of the bishop, whereof the minister to be one, and be laid up in the bishop's registry, there to be for a perpetual memory thereof.

88 Churches not to be profaned.

The churchwardens or questmen and their assistants shall suffer no plays, feasts, banquets, suppers, church ales, drinkings, temporal courts, or leets, lay juries, musters, or any other profane usage to be kept in the church, chapel or churchyard, neither the bells to be rung superstitiously upon holy days or eves abrogated by the book of common prayer, nor at any other times without good cause to be allowed by the minister of the place, and by themselves.

Bray, G., *The Anglican Canons 1529-1947*, COERS, *1998, 375-383.*

APPENDIX 7:
TIMESCALE PERTINENT TO THE SURVEY OF 1610

10 September 1610:

The Primary Visitation of Bishop Samuel Harsnett commenced with the Cathedral and then took in the four deaneries of the Archdeaconry of Chichester: Storrington, Boxgrove, Midhurst and Arundel. (Ep.I/18/30)

October – December 1610:

The courts dealt with a large number of cases and churchwardens regarding reported defects of churches that we now see as a response to a 'survey', such is the composition and sheer bulk of the cases. These court sessions were presided over by Francis Coxe or Roger Andrewes, always with Richard Juxon, Notary Public, in attendance. (Ep. I/17/13, ff.84-114)

January – April 1611:

Witnessed a number of cases that were signed off as churchwardens reported on repairs, given that many in the autumn were given until Christmas to report, while others had Easter, where repairs were expected to take longer. (Ep. I/17/13)

No evidence has been found of a comparable survey being conducted in the Archdeaconry of Lewes during this same period.

APPENDIX 8:
A PROCLAMATION FOR PREUENTING THE DECAYES OF CHURCHES AND CHAPPELS FOR THE TIME TO COME.

Issued by the King at Hampton Court, 11 October 1629

The Kings most Excellent Maiestie hauing of late taken special notice of the generall decayes and ruines of Parish Churches and Chappels in many parts of this Kingdom, and that by Law the same ought to be repaired and maintained from time to time, at the proper charge of the inhabitants and occupiers of Lands within those parishes and Chappelries respectively, who being altogether careless of their duties therein, haue in many places wilfully neglected the same, when with a little charge seasonably bestowed in time, they might easily preuent those great ruines, which afterwards grow more heauy to be supported by their own defaults, and sometimes those Churches and Chappels are by them purposely suffered to runne into such extreame ruin and decay out of hope to obtain some generall Collection, whereby to spare themselues, and to get the worke, which they are bound to doe by law, to be done by the common purse of others, such Collections hauing beene of late yeeres more frequently granted then heretofore.

His Maiestie therefore taking this matter into his Princely consideration, and holding it a great dishonour to our Christian profession, that the consecrated places of God's worship and Divine Service are no better looked unto, both by this Proclamation straitly charge and command all Archbishops, Bishops, Archdeacons, and others to whom it may appertaine, that they take speciall care, each of them within his owne limits and Jurisdiction, that this point of keeping and upholding the Churches and Chappels from time to time, in good, decent, and substantiall repaire, be exactly and duely performed, and therein not to rely upon the Churchwardens Presentments, who to sauue themselves and their neighbours from charge, will easily omit to make knowen the decayes of their Churches and their own defaults, but either by themselues in person, or by their Officials, as other persons of worth and trust, to take view and survey of the Churches and Chappels within their seuerall Jurisdictions, and where they find ought amisse, to cause the same to be speedily and carefully amended, and to limit and appoint set dayes for the doing thereof, that no needful worke be deferred too long, and to use the power of the Ecclesiastical Courts for putting the same in due execution. Willing and requiring also all his Maiesties Judges of the Common Law, to be very careful and wary, that in these cases which concern the repaire of Churches and Chappels according to His Maiesties Princely care and Royall commandment, the good worke undertaken in the Ecclesiastical Courts be not interrupted, by their too easy granting of Prohibitions, which, as with other cases, so especially in this, would not be granted, but upon weighty and great cause, and upon strict and due examination.

And to take away from the said Inhabitants and Land-holders of parishes, the hope which they haue heretofore had to relieue themseluves by publique Collections, as also to present the causeless burthening of His louing Subjects, not lyable by the Law to the said reparations, His Maiestie hereby doeth further charge and command the Lord Keeper of the Great Seale of England, that from hencefoorth no Letters Patent be granted, nor suffered to passe the Seale for any Collection for the repayring or new building of any Churches or Chappels, or the Steeples of the same, excepting only in case of casualtie by fire, or extraordinarie violence of Tempest, wherby the said Churches, Chappels, or Steeples, are suddenly, without the Parishioners default, so greatly deacyed, as the Inhabitants and Land-holders are not able without helpe of others, to repayre or new build the same.

All which His Maiestie doth will and command to bee from henceforth duely and strictly obserued, as wel by the said Lord Keeper for his part, as by the Archbishops, Bishops, Judges, and others for their parts, as they tender his Maiesties good pleasure and Royall Commandement, that the great inconuenience, and dishonour of suffering the houses of Gods worship and service, to run into ruine and decay amongst us, may be hereafter carefully preuented.

TNA: SP/45/10

APPENDIX 9:
EXTRACT FROM ARCHBISHOP LAUD'S GENERAL INSTRUCTIONS TO SIR NATHANIEL BRENT CONCERNING THE EXECUTION OF HIS METROPOLITICAL VISITATION ISSUED 22 FEBRUARY 1633/4.

7   To visit in, as many places as is usuall in every Diocess.

8   To enquire after such Impropriacions whose Cure is not well serued.

9   Diverse Churches ruined by inclosures.

10   Nor Schools to be kept in any Chancell.

11   A strict inquiry into the peculiars that are held by prebends or lay persons.

12   To take order that the Surpliss and other decent Ceremonyes of the Church be duly used.

13   To bring the ffontes to theyr ancyent place whereuver they are reomoued.

14   To enquire carefully how his Majesties Instructions are obserued.

15   To looke to the seats in all Cathedrall & Collegiate Churches.

16   Whereuer you fynd the Chancell seured from the Church or any other waye prophaned, to see it remedyed.

In a further memorandum in the same document, Laud issued advice on how his officials should conduct themselves during the visitation. He urged that they set a good example, 'bow at the blessed name of our Saviour' in services, and ensure that Communion Tables were not abused in use as a 'Checker to write' on or receive money, adding that should the officials need to write charges themselves, they should do so from 'one of the seats at the west end of the Chancell' and certainly not on the said Communion Table.

TNA: SP/16/260/90

APPENDIX 10:

TIMESCALE PERTINENT TO THE CHURCH SURVEY OF 1636

October 1629:

A Royal Proclamation called for better care of churches across the land and notably called for episcopal or archidiaconal surveys rather than reliance on the word of churchwardens.

May-July 1635:

Sir Nathaniel Brent was active in Sussex conducting a Metropolitical Visitation for Archbishop William Laud.

October 1635-April 1636:

Cases concerning glebe terriers, tables of degrees of marriage, communion cloth and registers occurred in high numbers in Chichester courts, presumably following up issues raised in the Metropolitical Visitation (Ep. I/17/26).

February 1635/6:

Orders were given to the Dean and Chapter of Chichester Cathedral based on the findings of the Archbishop's Visitation.

July-August 1636:

A run of church cases in Chichester courts highlighted communion table issues and the absence of tables of degrees of marriage in churches (Ep. I/17/25).

September 1636:

The Michaelmas Visitation of the Archdeacon was conducted.

November-December 1636:

Church surveys were reported to the Chichester church courts (Ep. 1/26/2).

June-July 1637:

Church cases were still being pursued & certificates required (Ep. 1/17/27).

APPENDIX 11:
EXTRACT FROM THE VISITATION ARTICLES EMPLOYED BY BISHOP MONTAGU AT CHICHESTER WITH MINOR VARIATIONS BETWEEN 1628 AND 1638
Articles concerning the church, the ornaments, sacred utensils and possessions of the same

1. Whether have you in your church, the whole bible of the largest volume, and last translation, the book of common prayer: the two bookes of homilies?

2. Have you a font of stone, for the administration of baptisme, set up in the usuall place neere the church doore, with a cover to keepe it from dust and soyle?

3. Have you a convenient, and decent communion table placed conveniently as it ought, with a carpet of silke, or some other comely stuffe to be layd upon it in time of divine service, and a cleane lynnen for the time of communion?

4. Is it prophaned at any time, by sitting on it, casting hattes, or cloakes upon it, writing, or casting up accompts, or any other indecent usage?

5. Have you in your church a convenient seat for your minister to reade divine service, and to preach in, a comely large, and fine surplice, a communion cup and flagon of silver or pewter; a chest for almes with three lockes and keyes, another chest for keeping the bookes, ornaments, and utensils of the church; have you a register booke in parchment for christnings, burialls, marriages, and are these duely and faithfully written and recorded therein or not, and is the same safely kept in a chest with three lockes and keyes according to the canon?

6. Whether is your church, chappell, chancell, sufficiently repayred, decently and comely kept, as well within as without, be the seats maintayned, the steeple and bels preserved, the windowes glased, the doore paved, and all things in such sort as may well beseeme the house of God?

7. Whether is your churchyard well mounded, and fenced, kept cleane without nusance, or soyle cast into it: is it incroached upon, and by whome? Doe any offensively keepe doores, outletts, or passages into your churchyard: doe any use to quarrell, fight, play, or make meetings, banquets, church-ales there, doe any keepe courts, leetes, lawdaies, musters there, or otherwise use it being a consecrated place, contrary to the 88 canon?

Visitation Articles and Injunctions of the Early Stuart Church II, ed. Fincham, K., Church of England Record Society, 5, 1998, 26.

APPENDIX 12:
TIMELINE COVERING EPISCOPAL & METROPOLITICAL VISITATIONS AFFECTING THE DIOCESE OF CHICHESTER BETWEEN 1600 AND 1641

In theory, **archidiaconal visitations** for Chichester and Lewes could have occurred at Easter and Michaelmas annually, hence around May and September each year. In practice, one was often missed out, particularly on occasions when, triennially, the bishop held a general visitation across the whole diocese. Metropolitical visitations (indicated in **bold**) were held for each archbishop in this period, and extended to all dioceses in his southern province. Primary visitations, held by a new bishop to the diocese, are indicated in **bold** as these might be expected to carry more weight with clergy and churchwardens. The list suggests that the diocese was quite closely monitored during this period.

1600	Bishop Watson's visitation in the autumn
1603	Bishop Watson's visitation in the autumn
	[1604 New Canons for the Church of England ratified by Convocation]
1605	**Archbishop Bancroft's Metropolitical Visitation in July**
1606	**Bishop Andrewes' primary visitation September-October**
1609	Bishop Andrewes' visitation in the autumn
1610	**Bishop Harsnett's primary visitation in the autumn**
1613	Bishop Harsnett's visitation in the autumn
1615	**Archbishop Abbot's Metropolitical Visitation in August-September**
1616	Bishop Harsnett's visitation in the autumn
1619	**Bishop Carleton's primary visitation in the autumn**
1622	Bishop Carleton's visitation in the autumn
1625	Bishop Carleton's visitation in the autumn
1628	**Bishop Montagu's primary visitation in the autumn**
1631	Bishop Montagu's visitation in the autumn
1634	Bishop Montagu's visitation in the autumn
1635	**Archbishop Laud's Metropolitical Visitation in May-July**
1637	Bishop Montagu's visitation in the autumn
1638	**Bishop Duppa's primary visitation in the autumn**
1641	Bishop Duppa's visitation in the autumn

INDEX OF NAMES

This Index lists the names of individuals recorded in the survey texts. These are mainly incumbents, patrons or impropriators/farmers; however, where individuals are named specifically in the text of the surveys, they are also indexed here.

Individuals referred to by title eg., Lord Lumley, are indexed. Individuals referred to by position eg., Dean, Archbishop of Canterbury, have been omitted. Where solely a surname is indexed eg., Chatfield, the text shows Mr Chatfield, etc.

Variant names have been conservatively grouped thus: Hutchenson/Hutchinson, where the strong likelihood is that the references are to the same individual. But those searching for names are advised to look for likely variants.